## JACKIE KAY
# BESSIE SMITH

Jackie Kay is the author of the memoir *Red Dust Road* as well as several critically acclaimed poetry collections— including *The Adoption Papers* (winner of the Scottish Arts Council Book Award), *Off Colour* (shortlisted for the T. S. Eliot Prize), and *Life Mask* (a Poetry Book Society Recommendation)—almost all of which were collected in *Darling: New & Selected Poems*. Her first novel, *Trumpet*, won the Guardian Fiction Prize and was shortlisted for the International Dublin Literary Award. A former National Poet of Scotland, she has also written several plays and children's books. She lives in Manchester, England.

## Other Works by Jackie Kay

# BESSIE SMITH

# BESSIE SMITH

*A Poet's Biography of a Blues Legend*

# JACKIE KAY

VINTAGE BOOKS
A Division of Penguin Random House LLC
New York

A VINTAGE BOOKS ORIGINAL, SEPTEMBER 2021

*Copyright © 1997, 2021 by Jackie Kay*

Library of Congress Cataloging-in-Publication Data
Names: Kay, Jackie, 1961– author.
Title: Bessie Smith : a poet's biography of a blues legend / Jackie Kay.
Description: Vintage books original edition. | New York :
Vintage Books, 2021. | Includes bibliographical references.
Identifiers: LCCN 2021005504 (print) | LCCN 2021005505 (ebook) |
ISBN 9780593314272 (trade paperback) | ISBN 9780593314289 (ebook)
Subjects: LCSH: Smith, Bessie, 1894–1937. | Singers—United States—
Biography. | Blues musicians—United States—Biography.
Classification: LCC ML420.S667 K393 2021 (print) | LCC ML420.S667
(ebook) | DDC 782.421643092 B—dc23
LC record available at https://lccn.loc.gov/2021005504
LC ebook record available at https://lccn.loc.gov/2021005505

**Vintage Books Trade Paperback ISBN: 978-0-593-31427-2**
**eBook ISBN: 978-0-593-31428-9**

www.vintagebooks.com

Printed in the United States of America
10  9  8  7  6  5  4  3  2  1

For my dear dad, John Kay (1925–2019),
who passed his love of Bessie on to me

Show me a hero and I will write you a tragedy.

F. Scott Fitzgerald

And freedom had a name. It was called the blues.

Walter Mosley

# CONTENTS

# THE RED GRAVEYARD

There are some stones that open in the night like flowers.
Down in the red graveyard where Bessie haunts her lovers.
There are stones that shake and weep in the heart of night.
Down in the red graveyard where Bessie haunts her lovers.

Why do I remember the blues?
I am five or six or seven in the back garden;
the window is wide open;
her voice is slow motion through the heavy summer air.
Jelly roll. Kitchen man. Sausage roll. Frying pan.

Inside the house where I used to be myself,
her voice claims the rooms. In the best room even,
something has changed the shape of my silence.
Why do I remember her voice and not my own mother's?
Why do I remember the blues?

My mother's voice. What was it like?
A flat stone for skitting. An old rock.
Long long grass. Asphalt. Wind. Hail.
Cotton. Linen. Salt. Treacle.
I think it was a peach.
I heard it down to the ribbed stone.

I am coming down the stairs in my parents' house.
I am five or six or seven. There is fat thick wallpaper
I always caress, bumping flower into flower.

She is singing. (Did they play anyone else ever?)
My father's feet tap a shiny beat on the floor.

Christ, my father says, that's some voice she's got.
I pick up the record cover. And now. This is slow motion.
My hand swoops, glides, swoops again.
I pick up the cover and my fingers are all over her face.
Her black face. Her magnificent black face.
That's some voice. His shoes dancing on the floor.

There are some stones that open in the night like flowers.
Down in the red graveyard where Bessie haunts her lovers.
There are stones that shake and weep in the heart of night.
Down in the red graveyard where Bessie haunts her lovers.

# BESSIE SMITH

# INTRODUCTION

There are some people whose voices ring out across the centuries, who, even after they have gone, possess a strange ability to still be effortlessly here. Bessie's voice has that quality. Unsettled most of her life, she still unsettles. Try to imagine asking her about anything that is going on today, from the floods, to the climate crisis, to the coronavirus, to the Black Lives Matter movement, to the Me Too movement, to the refugee crisis, and you would find an answer in her rich and resonant blues narratives. We could match any of today's troubles and anxieties to her music. The blues are not past. Bessie's blues are current.

Her narratives are even eerily prescient – she sang about floods, about sexual abuse, about financial crashes, about sudden changes in circumstances, changes in love. There isn't anything that life could currently throw at her that would surprise her. Her blues sought the truth – the truth in all its multiplicity; the hard truth, the strangest truth, the supernatural truth. The whole truth has a different ring to it in the world of Bessie's blues. In these surreal times, where distinguishing the truth is a challenge, Bessie's voice has a pure and true ring. She is telling it like it is. There's nothing fake about her. And because she was not afraid to bear witness to her times, to rising racism and the Ku Klux Klan, to inequalities and class differences, to hypocrisy and the dangers of celebrity, she also manages to bear witness to our times. Pioneers don't just lead the way in their own time; they continue to refract and reflect our time. Pioneers can perform the magic trick of being contemporary in any time.

For my twelfth birthday, my dad bought me my first double album. It was Bessie Smith's *Any Woman's Blues*. I was drawn to the two-sided picture of her on the cover, the smiling Bessie and the sorrowful one. It wasn't long before I made her part of my extended imaginary black family, before I felt not just as if she belonged to me, but as if I belonged to her. She felt like kith and kin. She felt like kindred. There was something in her that seemed to recognise something in me. Well, that's what we think with people whose writing or music or art we love – it is not so much that we see something in their work, but that we are deluded enough to imagine they might understand us, comprehend the complex workings of our minds. They feel like soul mates. We feel known, intimately known.

Now, more than twenty years since I first wrote about Bessie, that feeling is so ingrained in me that it feels a little awkward to state it. It feels like stating the obvious. I'm older now than she ever got to be, twenty years older, and yet trying to imagine her at fifty-seven or at seventy-seven is not all that difficult. Not difficult because the people you choose to accompany you don't die, they hold up one of life's oddly glinting mirrors. You're not the young girl that loved Bessie Smith any more and danced to the blues in your living room. You are a fifty-seven-year-old woman whose odd reflection in the waiting mirror perhaps Bessie would catch? You're not the same any more. You've changed physically, emotionally; you've learnt and unlearnt different things. But you still love Bessie. She is one of those folks you go to for comfort and understanding when the going gets rough, the rough gets going.

Bessie Smith is the perfect antidote to these times. She tells no lies. Her voice is still authentic. Her stories seem ever more urgent. She's still troubled. Her eyebrows still furrowed. Loving her blues, the exact timbre of her voice, no longer even feels like taste or choice. It goes deeper than that. I don't know what gave me the idea back in 1996 when I first wrote *Bessie* to write about my life and write about her life together. How odd to try and do both at the same time. I wasn't interested in writing a standard kind of biography. I think I was interested in how much our interests and passions form part of our own identity – how we beg and borrow and become ourselves, how much of a big mixture we are. I was interested in the point of intersection.

I was working on my novel *Trumpet* at the time when Nick Drake asked me if I would put on hold what I was writing and choose a gay icon to write about instead. It was strange. I was having trouble with *Trumpet* in trying to find the right tone to tell the story – and, strangely, returning to the blues and immersing myself in Bessie and in her contemporaries clarified the voice of *Trumpet*. I started to see the style of the book as a piece of music. The whole chapter called 'Music' in *Trumpet* was directly inspired by thinking about how the blues journeyed into jazz. I was trying to find a metaphor for that fluidity in our own gendered identities. I was thinking about how we imagine states of identity to be static when they are in fact fluid. I had arrived at the conclusion that my hero, Joss Moody, would be called 'he' after he made the decision to present himself to the world as a man, and that to refer to him as 'she' would be a kind of an affront. Writing about Bessie and her blues, about her very fluid identity, how she was as at home in pearls and plumes as in a man's suit, allowed me to create Joss Moody. The two books seem twinned. Writing about Bessie unleashed something and *Trumpet* kind of sprang to life.

Twenty-odd years on it is amazing how much has changed in a relatively short period of time. The shift in attitudes to gay and trans people has probably been the biggest social change of our lifetime. It is not to say that prejudice does not still exist – but still it would have been impossible to imagine all the terms that have so quickly become part of our new vocabulary; we have walked into a changing language about ourselves, which is still shifting, still open to question, still partly greeted with derision in places, but which none the less has reshaped the gendered landscape that we lived in just twenty years ago. I want every bit of it, Bessie sang.

I can see my dad, who died last year, sitting in his arm-chair singing 'Nobody Knows You When You're Down and

Out'. I can see him relishing the words – the notion that people are fickle and that capitalism is a sham. I can see the enjoyment of the philosophy that is in the blues. There is something egalitarian and equalising about the blues. There are salutary lessons to be found. There's a terrible reckoning in the space between 'once I lived' and now – and there's nobody to save you. Falling so low is something that might have been predicted. No place to go. It seemed to me, in the way that my dad sang Bessie, that everyone who had ever been poor without ever being rich could yet understand the falling from grace, and could empathise. Everyone might intuit the shallowness of the well-to-do. Might sympathise with the trauma of being left on your tod to cope with whatever after having had 'friends'. The story of the blues – Bessie's blues, going from something to nothing, from having happiness to being wretched, from having love to losing it, from being feted to being ignored – those terrible trajectories were all around us. They were real life. The reason that I loved the blues was because they didn't appear to me to be made up in any way. They sprang from life's source, life's true well and, well, they tapped into the well of loneliness on the way, allowed for a kind of transformation, a becoming. If you can recognise the other in you, the other side, then perhaps your life can be meaningful in some way you hadn't yet imagined.

Blues led the way. It's hard to think of so much music – jazz, rap, house – without the blues coming first. We can trace the etymology of the blues, the brilliant blues' bloodline and find it riveting, fascinating, like going onto a genealogy site and finding ancestors. The blues singers are the ancestral voice, the one that can be heard still – those hauntings, those defiant mournful calls. Bessie's blues are bang up to the minute. She calls and, across the years and miles, we respond.

# IN THE HOUSE OF THE BLUES

I was adopted in 1961 and brought up in a suburban house in a suburban street in the north of Glasgow. A small semi-detached Wimpey house. Outside our house is a cherry-blossom tree that is as old as me. It doesn't seem the most likely place to be introduced to the blues, but then blues travel to wherever the blues lovers go. In my street and in the neighbouring streets to Brackenbrae Avenue, I never saw another black person. There was my brother and me. That was it. The butcher, the baker and the candlestick maker were all white. (Although I never actually met a candlestick maker – has anyone?)

So the first time I saw Bessie Smith, it really was like finding a friend. I saw her before I heard her. My father – a Scottish communist who loved the blues – bought me my first double album. I was twelve. The album was called *Bessie Smith: Any Woman's Blues* and produced by CBS Records ( John Hammond and Chris Albertson; Albertson went on to write her biography). I remember taking the album off him and poring over it, examining it for every detail. Her image on the cover captivated me. She looked so familiar. She looked like somebody I already knew in my heart of hearts. I stared at the image of her, trying to recall who it was she reminded me of.

She looked so sorrowful and so strong. She would stand

up for herself, so she would. She wouldn't take any insults from people. I could see from her eyes that she was a fighter. I put her down and I picked her up. I stroked her proud, defiant cheeks. I ran my fingers across her angry eyebrows. I soothed her. Sometimes I felt shy staring at her, as if she was somehow able to see me looking. On the front cover she was smiling. Every feature of her face lit up by a huge grin bursting with personality. Her eyes full of hilarity. Her wide mouth full of laughing teeth. On the back she was sad. Her mouth shut. Eyes closed. Eyebrows furrowed. The album cover was like a strange two-sided coin. The two faces of Bessie Smith. I knew from that first album that I had made a friend for life. I would never forget her.

The names of the blues songs transported me places, created scenes and visions. 'Jail House Blues', 'Haunted House Blues', 'Eavesdropper's Blues', 'Graveyard Dream Blues', 'Whoa, Tillie, Take Your Time', 'St Louis Gal', 'New Orleans Hop Scop Blues', 'Kitchen Man', 'Chicago Bound Blues', 'Worn Out Papa Blues'. Each name was enough to make up a story. That's what I liked about the blues, they told stories. The opposite of fairy tales; these were grimy, real, appalling tragedies. There were people dying in the blues; people coming back to haunt the people who were living in the blues; there were bad men in the blues; there were wild women in the blues. People travelled places, or wished they were someplace else in the blues. Could I be a St Louis Gal? Or could I be Tillie? Might Chicago be a place I would go when I grew up? Was the New Orleans Hop Scop like hopscotch? There were Daddys and Mamas galore in the blues. Every next person was a Mama or a Daddy but they didn't sound like my mum and dad. 'Mistreating Daddy, mistreating Mama all the time.' People got drunk and ate pigs' feet in the blues. It was totally wild.

We had an old-fashioned record player that looked as if it was pretending to be a bit of furniture until you lifted its lid and saw its strange black arm and needle. I'd place the record down into the player, lift the arm of the needle and try and get it on the exact line of my favourite track. Sometimes I'd miss and hear the end of another unfamiliar track that would, for a moment, make me want to listen to it. I liked the way the piano and the horn sounded comical, as if they weren't taking any of this so seriously. Especially in songs like 'Cemetery Blues' and 'Graveyard Dream Blues'; the musical accompaniment sounded like it was all one big joke, like the funny music in silent movies.

My favourite of the lot was 'Dirty No-Gooder's Blues'. It sounded so bad. The very name made you think things you weren't supposed to be thinking at that age. A Dirty No-Gooder? What was he? Some man that said filthy words and had no morals. Some man who could not be good; some man who dedicated his whole life to being bad. I found the blues so exciting because the characters were real 'characters'; people who behaved badly, who did terrible things, who killed and murdered and went to prison and missed Chicago and wanted to 'Take it right back to the place where you got it', whatever the 'it' was. The men in the blues were lowdown and rotten, cheating and lying and lazy.

There's nineteen men living in my neighbourhood.
There's nineteen men living in my neighbourhood.
Eighteen of them are fools and the one ain't no doggone good.

'Dirty No-Gooder's Blues'

At the age of twelve in my small suburban neighbourhood, the idea of describing men in this way was scandalous, hilarious. Mr Aird, Mr Tweedie, Mr Dunsmore, Mr Macintosh, Mr Murray, Mr Kerr, Mr Cochrane. Which one was no doggone good? Whenever I listened to the lyrics of the blues they made me feel I was being entrusted with a secret. I was being told a secret story about some no-good, no-count man. The story was for me and not for him. The story was a joke on him. Bessie Smith was singing for women. It was women who were singing those blues and the lyrics were mainly about the 101 ways a man could let you down. I guess I took the warning. Every woman could understand the blues. That's why this album was called *Any Woman's Blues*.

I realised that I could choose always to have Bessie Smith in my life, that she was not going to betray me or go off with another friend, or move to Kirkintilloch, or suddenly turn nasty. Nobody could take her away from me. And when I grew up and went away, I could take her with me. And I did. Hours and hours looking at her face on the cover and many hours memorising the lyrics to the songs. They weren't all blues; some were vaudeville, some were Tin Pan Alley. But everything Bessie Smith sang sounded like a blues song. I had my favourite songs that I would play over and over again. 'Kitchen Man', 'Dirty No-Gooder's Blues', 'I'm Wild About That Thing', 'He's Got Me Goin''.

> Got me goin'
> He's got me goin'
> But I don't know where I'm headed for!

When I listened to the songs on this first album, I always assumed that they were about Bessie Smith's own life. (It didn't occur to me to think this of folk, soul or rock singers.) The blues sounded like autobiography, like ordinary people telling the story of their lives. There was always an I in the blues. It was all first person. When I listened to 'Nobody Knows You When You're Down and Out' and 'Wasted Life Blues', I felt so sad for Bessie Smith. I could picture her whole life suddenly changing. (Her whole life did change, strangely mirroring 'Nobody Knows You'; she might as well have been singing about herself.) I felt so passionate about her, it made me angry. I'd listen to the lyrics of her songs and that voice of hers that no other voice can ever come near:

Nobody knows you
When you're down and out.
In my pocket, not one penny
And my friends, I haven't any,
But if I ever get on my feet again
Then I'll meet my long-lost friend.
It's mighty strange without a doubt
Nobody knows you when you're down and out,
I mean when you're down and out.

I'd imagine her, wandering through the streets of segregated America, penniless, friendless. *Down and out.* There were many down-and-outs in Glasgow on Sauchiehall Street on a Saturday night. If nobody loved Bessie Smith when she was down and out, then nobody would love me. All that was left then would be to dream of death. Graveyard Dream Blues. Cemetery Blues. Wasted Life Blues. Somehow being down and out in America seemed to be inextricably linked with her colour. I could not separate them. I could not separate myself. I am the same colour as she is, I thought to myself, electrified. I am the same colour as Bessie Smith. I am not the same colour as my mother, my father, my grandmother, my grandfather, my friends, my doctor, my dentist, my butcher, my teacher, my headmaster, my next-door neighbour, my aunt, my uncle, my mother's friends, my father's friends. The shock of not being like everyone else; the shock of my own reflection came with the blues. My own face in the mirror was not the face I had in my head.

a bit nonplussed when I discovered that all those jelly rolls and sugar rolls in those songs had nothing to do with food.

What was it she reminded me of? Whenever I impersonated her in front of my mirror with my hairbrush microphone, I had a sense of something, at the edge of myself, that I mostly ignored; the first awareness of myself being black. I'd only ever think about it if something reminded me. Bessie Smith always reminded me. I am the same colour as Bessie Smith. I'd look at her hands then I'd look at my own hands. I'd look at her nose then I'd look at my own nose. Perhaps she is related after all. Maybe my great-great-grandmother was a blues singer. Who knows? The great thing about being adopted was that you could invent your family all the time. You could make them up and invent yourself in the process. At one point, every time I saw Shirley Bassey on the telly singing 'Goldfinger', I was convinced she was my birth mother. Any time I came across a black person, usually on TV, or in a book, or on a political poster that my father brought home, I tried to work out their relationship to me. I concocted an imaginary black family for myself through images that I had available to me. There were a lot of images in this politically internationalist household. Nelson Mandela, Angela Davis, the Soledad Brothers, Cassius Clay, Count Basie, Duke Ellington. I liked trying to connect one black person to another, a racial jigsaw puzzle. I was aware that racial discrimination existed all over the world. South Africa had sixteen legal definitions of black; South Africa had borrowed its system of apartheid from the American South. At Christmas time, I would sit down with my mum and send cards to the political prisoners in South Africa. All black people could at some point in their life face racism or racialism (I could never understand the difference) therefore all black people had a common bond. It was like sharing blood.

I did not think that Bessie Smith only belonged to African Americans or that Nelson Mandela belonged to South Africans. I could not think like that because I knew then of no black Scottish heroes that I could claim for my own. I reached out and claimed Bessie.

When I was a young girl, Bessie Smith comforted me, told me I was not alone, kept me company. I could imagine her life as I invented my own; I would not have grown up in the same way without her. Just at that crucial moment, before my periods, after my first bra, before I had any big romance, before I went to secondary school, there she was. It was perfect timing. I was just the right age for her to become my lifelong friend, my beautiful flame, my brave heart-throb, my paragon of virtue. My libidinous, raunchy, fearless blueswoman. My righteous, courageous, wild blueswoman. I am still full of her passion. I have her spark in my eye. I can burn with love, burn with the blues. I am still totally, utterly, Wild About That Thing.

I heard the singing of the Mississippi when Abe Lincoln went down to New Orleans, and I've seen its muddy bosom turn all golden in the sunset.

I've known rivers:
Ancient, dusky rivers.

My soul has grown deep like the rivers.

Langston Hughes, 'The Negro Speaks of Rivers'

# CHATTANOOGA, 1894

According to the date on her marriage certificate, Bessie Smith was born in Chattanooga, Tennessee on 15 April 1894. But we cannot be sure. Chris Albertson tells us that 'Southern bureaucracy made little distinction between its black population and its dogs; such official records as a birth certificate were not always considered necessary.'[1] But Chattanooga it was, definitely. Not any of the other towns close by: Knoxville, Nashville, Birmingham, Atlanta, Oak Ridge, Blue Ridge, Scottsboro.

What does a girl from Bishopbriggs near Glasgow know about Chattanooga? She might have heard that song: *Pardon me boy, is that the Chattanooga Choo-choo? / Track 29, well you can give them a shine.* But that's about it. I looked up Chattanooga in my atlas. Chattanooga, Hamilton County, Tennessee. It made me feel even closer to her being able to find it in the atlas, to rest my finger on the town; it covered the whole of it. There's a certain satisfaction to be had from finding a place in an atlas. The next best thing to going there. With my finger pressing into the name Chattanooga, I tried to picture it. Well, it wasn't like Glasgow. It wouldn't be like anywhere I had been. It might look like a town in a Western. Maybe. It would have a small railway station where the trains coming in and out of Chattanooga were a major event, a happening. The train would make a huge boasting noise as it came into the station, announcing its arrival. People with their collars turned up would be waiting in the cold wind. *There's gonna be a certain party at the station / Satin and lace – I used to call funny face.* What else? A sheriff. A sheriff's hat. Dust. Horses. Poor black people living in shacks. A river. A long, long river that passes through practically every town in Tennessee. The Tennessee River. I traced it with my finger. The shape of a U. Parsons, Savannah, Decatur, Guntersville, Jasper, Chattanooga, Cleveland, Charleston, right up to Oak Ridge. *Dinner in the diner. Nothing could be finer / Than to have your ham and eggs in Carolina.* It was a bigger river than I could imagine. It was a dangerous river that could cause massive floods. A picture of people floating with furniture in the water rose up in my mind. A giant of a river.

Chattanooga, 1894. The sheriff would have a gun and a gun holster, wouldn't he? He would be white, definitely. He would be able to arrest a black man for just looking at him straight in the eye. A black man would have to keep his eyes down on the dusty street if he wanted to be safe. Someone new in town would be noticed. Chattanooga, 1894. The town would be packed with preachers. Many big brothers and big sisters. Large and lean religious people, black and white, the faces of people captured by religion. The white faces – pointed, pinched, spiteful. The black faces animated, arrested, actorish. Hymns, psalms, prayers, spirituals. 'Go Down, Moses', 'Swing Low, Sweet Chariot'. Bessie Smith would have gone to church as a young girl. (Church continued to play an important role in her life. She would often go after a heavy night's drinking!) The emotion of those songs – 'O Mary, Don't You Weep', 'Rough Rocky Road' – might have influenced the way she sang the blues.

Rough, rocky road, I'se most done suffering.
Rough, rocky road, I'se most done suffering.
Rough, rocky road, I'se most done suffering.
I'm bound to carry my soul to de Lord.
I'm bound to carry my soul to de Lord.

The preacher man would be the town's salvation. He would wear a white shirt and a black hat. In the black church the preacher man would get his congregation worked up till they were almost crazy with love for God. They would sing those spirituals the way Bessie Smith sang the blues, with total and utter belief and conviction. The Lord could lift them up and carry them away from the terrors and indignities of racism.

Bessie Smith was born into a place and a time where racist violence was in the air she breathed. In the name of a town. All over the South that Bessie loved were towns plagued by racism. The names of those places still ring with trauma. (We have our own traumatic town names in Scotland; we know the impact of just hearing the word Dunblane or Lockerbie.) The South is full of names of towns that make you sink and reel with disbelief. Birmingham, Alabama, where the black children were bombed in church. Scottsboro where nine innocent black men were accused of raping a white woman; eight of them were sent to the electric chair.

We have been sentenced to die for something we ain't never done. Us poor boys been sentenced to burn up on the electric chair for the reason that we is workers – and the color of our skin is black.

The Scottsboro boys

All over the South that Bessie Smith so loved are the graves of people murdered for being black. The blues never shied away from singing about tragedy. Later, Billie Holiday would sing about a lynching in 'Strange Fruit':

Southern trees bear a strange fruit,
Blood on the leaves and blood at the root,
Black bodies swaying in the Southern breeze,
Strange fruit hanging from the poplar trees.

The poet who wrote 'Strange Fruit', Lewis Allan, took it to Billie Holiday in 1939, two years after the death of Bessie Smith. When Lady Day first read the words of 'Strange Fruit', she didn't know what to make of it. But the song made such an impact on people that she later claimed to have written it herself. It became her song. 'Strange Fruit' provoked a huge reaction from its audience. Song and memory intertwined like branch and leaf. People in the audience would weep when they heard it, some would remember having witnessed lynchings themselves. Donald Clarke, in his biography of Billie,[2] tells us that:

> One evening . . . a woman followed Lady into the powder room crying, 'Don't you dare ever sing that song again. Don't you dare . . .' When she was seven or eight years old she had witnessed a lynching in the South.

Blues songs and real life weren't all that separate. These songs were not simple entertainment. They told terrible true stories. In the collection *American Negro Folk Songs* there is a disturbing little song about Chattanooga:

> Chattanooga, chickamauga,
> Tobe Domingus,
> Kill a nigger;
> I'm Alabama bound.

Reported in 1915 from Auburn, Alabama. Tobe Domingus was the name of a policeman from the nearby city of Dothan who killed a black man. Bessie Smith would have been twenty-one around this time. This song actually records that incident. Songs like this give us a kind of history we don't find in the books. One way of dealing with racism was to write and sing songs about it. There is so much healthy irony in these songs. Bessie would have grown up hearing those songs.

Chattanooga, 1894 – 138 miles southeast of Nashville. The town grew with the coming of the railroads in the middle of the nineteenth century. By 1900, Chattanooga had a population of thirty thousand, over half of it black. Unemployment was high. Opportunities for black workers were few. In fact there were two. You could either be an ill-paid manual or domestic labourer or you could join a travelling show.

Bessie Smith was one of eight children. Her father, William Smith, was a part-time Baptist preacher who ran a small mission. He died soon after Bessie was born. One of her brothers had died in infancy before she was born. Her family lived in crushing poverty. Bessie lived in what she later described as 'a little ramshackle cabin', where the rats outnumbered the children. A one-room wooden shack on Charles Street in the Blue Goose Hollow section of Chattanooga. Her mother, Laura Smith, was dead by the time Bessie was eight. Another brother died around the same time as her mother. With no adults to earn money or care for them, the Smith children had to do it for themselves. Viola, Bessie's elder sister, took on the main responsibility to make ends meet, taking in laundry which she boiled on top of an outdoor coal stove. She looked after the surviving Smiths – Bessie, Tinnie, Lulu, Andrew and Clarence. From the age of nine Bessie sang for nickels – maybe a dime once in a blue moon – on Chattanooga's Ninth Street, a stretch along which the city's black night-life centred. Her brother Andrew accompanied her on the guitar. Sometimes they would stay in their own neighbour-hood, in front of the White Elephant Saloon on Thirteenth and Elm. From a very early age, singing was literally her survival. It helped to feed her and her family. When any-one threw a coin, she would say, 'That's right, give to the church.'

I can just about see her at the age of nine standing on a street corner singing for a nickel or a dime. She is tall for her age, and big-boned. She already has a mature sense of herself and a deep voice. Any song suits her. She can sing anything. What did she sing? A spiritual? Something like this:

Oh! brudder, can't you hol' out yo' light,
Oh! brudder, can't you hol' out yo' light,
Oh! brudder, can't you hol' out yo' light,
An' let yo' light shine ober de world.

She would have stood out in the cold, inadequately clothed, singing whatever it was she sang. Perhaps it was a spiritual, perhaps it was a work song.

Born in no'th Carlina,
Raised in Tennessee,
Worked like hell in Georgia,
Died in Germinee.

Whatever it was she sang, her voice even then would have attracted attention. You've got to be born with a voice like that. A voice like that doesn't come along often. Passers-by must have noticed. She made more nickels than her brothers or her sisters. Even at this early age, she was the main breadwinner.

*One thing I notice about maself – I can sing when the sky is a certain way, hanging down low and mean and grey, looking as threatening as Ma could look sometimes. When the sky is like that, the songs come out more gutsy. I am a gutsy girl ain't nobody ever gonna run me down. Ma sistah Viola wants some meat this Satday. We gets meat once in a blue moon. When the sky is all moody blues, I holler ma songs here on the corner like I'm warning people about themselves or something. People stop and listen. I know people are always gonna stop and listen to me. I got that sense about maself. Ma mama done dead. Ma papa done dead. He was always saying, 'If it's the last thing I do before I die.' Ma mama said he said it so much, he made himself die. The last thing he did, she said was try and fix the door of our cabin 'cause the big storm had done damaged it and the wind was coming into our dreams at night. We was always cold and hungry. Ma father was good at catching rats and killing them. Viola says he would hold the dead rat up in the air by its tail and say, 'Gotcha.' I ain't nevah known nothin' else but being po'. I nevah owned a pair of ma own shoes. I seen girls on the other side with dresses on, but I ain't nevah had a new dress. All my clothes are nothing but rags. But that's not bothering me. I know I'm gonna have me a nice dress one day. I just knows it. Viola laughs violent when I say such things. She tells me I'm strange and not like the rest of them. 'What you talking about I'm not the same!' I want to hit Viola when she says shit like that. I feel like I'm a grown woman already, but I'm no different from the rest of them. I want to be the same as the rest of my family. Maybe I is different. I know I sing different. Do singing different make the whole of me different? I know I gets these moods — coming in at me just like weather. They catch me and they knock me right down, my whole face like the devil himself is sitting inside me cooking up some pigs' feet. Ma eyebrows arch themselves like bows and arrows. I talk dirty and I'm only nine. But I don't really think of myself as only nine. I nevah like to laugh when Viola or Andrew tease me. I feel like dying when I hear the sound of mocking laughter. It eats on my insides and makes me evil. I go straight up and I grab hold of them. I knock them down, batter them with my fists till I hear them whimper. Don't care who they are. Ain't nobody gonna run me down. When my temper is hot, not even a whole ocean of cold water gonna cool that temper down. I could catch a chicken and wring its scrawny neck. If they say sorry enough times to me, I just might calm down. Viola say, 'Bessie, that temper of yours is gonna get you into trouble someday.' I know that's true but there ain't a thing I can do about it.*

*Mama died because she was poor. She didn't get enough. She didn't get enough of anything and she gone and died.*

*I gonna help my family if it's the last thing I do before I die. When the sky is all hung down low, like a bony dog, slithering and insinuating itself about the neighbourhood, I can hear something come out of me, something that's inside me come out. And the more the roar comes out of me, the more folk gather round me on the corner. I heard someone say, Listen to that girl sing. Listen to her. I was standing there listening to myself. I could hear it myself. I ain't stupid. I know I can sing. I know I sing like nobody else in the whole goddam world. And that's the truth. I just knows myself. One day I'm gonna be somebody big. And that sister of mine better bow her sweet head. I'm gonna have so much fun telling her I told you so. I'm gonna get me a fine dress and a pair of shoes. Just imagine these dirty dusty feet of mine going into a pair of sweet little shoes. Little black shiny shoes. I'm sure a shop in the town might have a pair when I'm ready. I nevah go that way. I nevah really been out of this here Blue Goose Hollow.*

*Goose Hollow is called Goose Hollow because everybody who lives here is hungry, hollow bellies. Can't get no bird or animal to eat. No goose, no chicken, no pig, no cow. We eat the scraps here. The bits that other neighbourhoods throw away. That's what Andrew tole me. But Tinnie say that's a lie. Tinnie say it's called Goose Hollow because one day after the big rains a whole flock of geese descended in the hollow there near the water. They all marched along following their mama like they had some purpose in life and then suddenly stopped. Well those geese nevah flew after that day, nevah went anywhere. They just stayed in that there Goose Hollow like they'd found their Mecca. So say Tinnie. But Viola, now she say, that's just about as much rubbish as she ever heard. It's called Goose Hollow because old Sam's grandfather was asked by the bossman where he lived and his mind went blank because Goose Hollow use ta be called the Belly, but he didn't want ta say 'I live in the Belly' to his bossman. Sam looked up to the sky and saw a goose flapping its fat wings, a big one, so he just come up with Goose Hollow. And when he came back that night after working in that white man's yard he laughed and told everyone the name of where they lived. And everyone thought it was funny. Goose Hollow. It stuck. It stuck 'cause the folk are stuck and ain't flying no place. I believe Viola. I've told Viola I'm going. I'm gonna be one bird that does fly out of here even if it means making my own wings. I'll be sure not to fly too close to the sun.*

The blues began in the South and spread their wings. Soon Bessie Smith's taxing tours could make a blues map of the country. There were favourite spots all over America where blues lovers, a lot of them migrant workers from the South, congregated. Hearing the blues in New York reminded the black Southerners of back home tongue. Smith would travel all over America, to Philadelphia, New York, Detroit, Cleveland, Memphis, New Orleans, Washington, Pittsburgh, Cincinnati, Kansas City. It was impossible to be a blues singer in the America of the 1920s without travel being in the blood. She never spent any of her money on making a home. She had no real concept of an adult home, which is probably why her childhood one continued to mean so much to her. Her home as an adult was on the road, travelling all over America, becoming particularly intimate with the backstreet bars in different towns. She always knew a place to go where she could get wildly drunk.

But Chattanooga tugged at the heart, the way the place you are born in always does. Just seeing the landscape around there made her feel at home. She liked travelling in the South. She liked the folk of the South. She didn't like those 'uppity northern bitches'. The people in the North were all pretence. The people in the South were real, genuine. It was all in the cooking. The people in the North couldn't cook worth a damn. She had to return home to get a decent meal. She always preferred to do her own cooking even on the road; perhaps this gave her some sense of 'home'. If she could take her favourite foods and her favourite drinks around with her wherever she went, then she could be at home anywhere. She liked cooking up big stews. Being from the South, she loved Coca-Cola. (She might have been addicted to the sugar in Coca-Cola to substitute for corn liquor.) There was something about the South, about coming from the South, that filled her with longing. Nostalgia, homesickness. Good chicken, chitterlings, boiled with scallions, dipped in flour and fried. Cornbread, collards, rice and peas, you could fill the hole of homesickness with a good gravy. Bessie Smith never forgot the girl she had been even when she became rich and famous. She never turned her back on her past and pretended that the girl standing on Chattanooga's Ninth Street singing for a nickel and a dime had never existed. Her voice kept its incredible power to haunt and disturb us because she never denied that girl. Even when she was rich and famous and dressed in ermine coats, she disliked black people who put on airs and graces, who were what she called 'dicty' blacks. She never changed. She stayed faithful to herself, to the girl she was who didn't have enough money for food or clothes. Maybe if she hadn't been born with that big voice of hers, she would have stayed in Chattanooga and barely ever moved from that town on the river. *She's gonna cry until I tell her that I'll never roam, so Chattanooga Choo-choo, won't you Choo-choo me home!*

I was thinking about Ma Rainey
Wonder where could Ma Rainey be.
I've been looking for her
Even been in old Tennessee.

Memphis Minnie, 'Ma Rainey'

# IN THE MA'S FOOTSTEPS

> She was the voice of the South, singing of the South,
> to the South.
>
> Edward Lucie-Smith, of Ma Rainey

Bessie was seventeen when she joined the Moses Stokes Travelling Show in 1912. The show was playing in a Chattanooga storefront. Her brother Clarence, who had been with travelling troupes since 1904, got her her first audition. It is possible she would have never been in show business if it hadn't been for Clarence.

Performing represented virtually the only alternative to sharecropping and manual labour for the poor and the black. (Will Friedwald tells us that Ethel Waters 'came to showbiz only as an escape from the grimiest of scullery work'.[3]) W. C. Handy, the so-called 'Father of the Blues' (because he was the first to write and popularise a blues composition – 'Memphis Blues', 1912), snapped up the opportunity to join a travelling minstrel show:

> It goes without saying that minstrels were a
> disreputable lot in the eyes of a large section of upper-
> crust Negroes . . . but it was also true that all the
> best talent of that generation came down the same
> drain. The composers, the singers, the musicians, the

speakers, the stage-performers – the minstrel shows got them all. For my part there wasn't a moment's hesitation . . . I took the break for what it was. The cards were running up my way at last.[4]

The very origin of minstrel shows is inextricably connected with racism. They began around the 1830s with white people wearing 'blackface' make-up and went on to become the most popular form of American entertainment through most of the nineteenth century. Burnt cork was applied to actors' faces to make them into caricature black people. Thomas Rice was the first white person to copy a black act; he'd seen an old black man in Cincinnati performing alone for his own amusement in an awkward dance (he was disabled) and singing a strange song:

Weel about, and turn about
And do jis so.
Ebry time I weel about
I jump Jim Crow.[5]

'Jim Crow' later became the term used for the laws of the segregating South.

Minstrelsy was a crude copying game. White actors created black caricatures and played them to the hilt, the Sambos and Zip Coons and Jim Dandys. All grotesque characters and simpletons that didn't possess a brain in their curly head. Minstrelsy distorted authentic

African-American folk music, dance, speech and style. Yet it was the black people's entertainment the whites were copying. W. C. Handy maintained that every plantation had its talented band that could crack jokes, and sing and dance to the accompaniment of banjo and bones. It is ironic that when black people themselves wanted to enter the world of showbiz towards the end of the nineteenth century, they often wore the burnt cork on their faces too. Black on black. As if it wasn't possible to be a genuine black face in entertainment; you had to wear some kind of mask.

Real black faces were not wanted for a very long time, and even today black actors get very few parts – there are few black faces to be seen on television and film apart from a handful of stars. It is possible to watch one Woody Allen film after another and not see a single black face. Irving C. Miller, who threw Bessie out of his chorus line in 1912 for being 'too black', was a product of his time as well. Black-skinned girls were not considered as beautiful as brown-skinned girls. In fact black girls weren't considered beautiful at all.

Like W. C. Handy, Bessie wouldn't have hesitated to join the Stokes show. The opportunity was a godsend. It offered her freedom from stultifying poverty. It gave her a chance to grow. The troupe was managed by Lonnie and Cora Fisher, and Bessie later cited Cora Fisher as a major influence, though there is no information about exactly how she influenced her. Perhaps she was the first person to give Bessie a belief in her own performing abilities. Perhaps she taught her essential performing tips that she never forgot.

Or she was simply kind to her, one of the first adults who was ever kind to her. Perhaps she was her salvation, saving her from a grim life. Maybe when Bessie looked back on her life, she always saw Cora Fisher at the helm, the woman who launched, wittingly or unwittingly, one of the biggest careers in blues history.

Although Bessie was initially taken on by Moses Stokes as a dancer, she soon began to sing the blues. She left Chattanooga for the first time to travel the South. With her in the troupe were Ma and Pa Rainey, who were dubbed 'the Assassinators of the Blues'. She moved on from Moses Stokes to join Irving C. Miller's tent show in 1913, until she was thrown out for being too dark. Later that same year, she was performing at the 81 Theatre in Atlanta, where actor Leigh Whipper saw her: 'She was just a teenager, and she obviously didn't know the artist she was. She didn't know how to dress – she just sang in her street clothes – but she was such a natural, she could wreck anybody's show.'[6] As a singer and dancer, she teamed up with Buzzin' Burton (as 'Smith & Burton') in Park's Big Revue at the Dixie Theatre, Atlanta, in 1914. And in 1915 she joined another travelling show, again with Ma Rainey – Fat Chappelle's Rabbit Foot Minstrels. She toured with the Rabbit Foots through the South in 1915 and also with Pete Werley's Florida Cotton Blossoms Minstrel Show, Silas Green's Minstrel Show and others in 1916.

The Rabbit Foot company was particularly popular in the Mississippi Valley, from where it drew many of its cast. Paul Oliver in his book *Songsters and Saints* quotes an advertisement:

'100 Performers and Musicians WANTED. Both ladies and gentlemen for my 2 shows under canvas. A Rabbit's Foot Comedy & Funny Folks Comedy. 40 weeks engagement for the right parties . . .' These shows were on the road in 1929–30 when the Alabama Minstrels, Jordan's Swiftfoot Minstrels, Richard's and Pringle's Georgia Minstrels, J. F. Murphy's Georgia Minstrels, The Fashion Plate Minstrels, Warner and Moorman's Famous Brown Derby Minstrels and John Van Arnam's Minstrels were all playing the South and Midwest . . . Many featured celebrated show singers: Lizzie Miles with the Alabama Minstrels, Bessie Smith with Irving C. Miller's show, Butterbeans and Susie with the Cole Brothers' Carnival.[7]

The minstrel troupes and blues travelling shows were often booked by TOBA (the Theatre Owners' Booking Association, aka Tough on Black Asses). They sang comedy songs and ballads and performed dramatic routines in addition to singing the blues. They mixed the rural blues tradition with the more sophisticated fare of the vaudeville stage. Humphrey Lyttelton in *The Best of Jazz* points out: 'Few "classic" blues singers of note became famous without serving a tough apprenticeship in the tent shows, barn-storming from settlement to township to plantation.'

Ida Cox (born Ida Prather) ran away from home to tour with White and Clark's Black and Tan Minstrels (as a blackface 'Topsy'). And she, along with Bessie Smith, Ma Rainey and many others, toured the theatre circuits from 1910 with the Rabbit Foot Minstrels, Silas Green from New Orleans and the Florida Cotton Blossoms. Ida Cox was often billed as 'The Sepia Mae West' – an unimaginable billing for Smith, who would be known as the Empress.

For Bessie, the difference between singing on Ninth Street with her brother accompanying her on guitar and travelling the South with a whole entourage of talented people must have been mind–blowing. Even later in her life when she could have afforded not to travel all over the place, she continued to do so. The exhilarating freedom of being on the road and arriving at completely new places with a whole group of people who knew how to have a good time made her into a lifelong travel addict. Travel was in her bones and in her blues. Places influenced the songs she wrote: 'Backwater Blues', 'Hot Springs Blues', 'Long Old Road', 'Lonesome Desert Blues', 'Dixie Flyer Blues'.

> Hold that engine, let sweet Mama get on board
> 'Cause my home ain't here, it's a long way down the road
> On that choo-choo, Mama's gonna find a berth
> Going to Dixieland, it's the grandest place on earth
> Dixie flyer, come on and let your drivers roll
> Wouldn't see us now to save nobody's doggone soul.
>                               'Dixie Flyer Blues'

This song has the sound of the train comically all the time in the background, the whistle and the chug-chugging of the engine. Travel in her blues, as in her real life, was a metaphor for getting away from men. Many of the blues she sang contained this restless desire to be on the road, going to someplace else. Either it's the man she loved who has just left this town, or it's Bessie herself who is leaving to get away from him. 'Florida Bound Blues', 'Nashville Women's Blues', 'Chicago Bound Blues', 'Far Away Blues', 'Gulf Coast Blues'. Going places, going anywhere was freedom. Bessie Smith grew up on the road, became intimate with places she passed through. It was all happening on the road. Sally Placksin, in her book *Jazzwomen*, says:

> Travelling by Pullman car, bus, or automobile, the most
> famous of the minstrel troupes – the Rabbit Foots,
> Florida Cotton Blossoms, Georgia Smart Set, Silas
> Green of New Orleans – would hit the cane brakes
> and the factory towns, the theaters of the bigger cities,
> laying down a bedrock of blues among the people. They
> followed the tobacco crops in the spring, the cotton
> crops in the fall, hit the coal mines and the Sea Islands
> off Georgia, arriving in each town at the season when
> the people had the most money to spend and were
> ready to go out and party. When the troupes arrived,
> the tents would go up, the bands would march through
> town, flyers would be handed out, and soon the show
> would be on . . .[8]

The company on the troupes was as exciting as the towns themselves. Ma Rainey was on that very first troupe Bessie ever joined, the Moses Stokes Travelling Show. Ma Rainey is now known as the 'Mother of the Blues'. She was the first of the blueswomen; all the rest followed her. She is the earliest link between the male country blues artists who wandered the streets of the South and the 'classic blues' women singers. Bessie Smith, Clara Smith, Mamie Smith and Laura Smith, Ida Cox, Victoria Spivey, Alberta Hunter, Sippie Wallace, Lizzie Miles, Bertha 'Chippie' Hill, Memphis Minnie Douglas – all owed a debt to Ma. Ma Rainey was born Gertrude Pridgett on 26 April 1886. Her father, Thomas Pridgett, and her mother, Ella Allen, were both minstrel troupers. Gertrude was one of five children baptised in the First African Baptist Church, Columbus, Georgia. She was already working as early as 1900 in a talent show, *A Bunch of Blackberries*, at Springer Opera House, and in 1902 she was singing blues songs on the road, long, long before W. C. Handy wrote his famous 'St Louis Blues' in 1914. The gold-toothed Ma Rainey was there before him (Humphrey Lyttelton describes her mouth as 'revealing in a broad grin a veritable Fort Knox of gold fillings') and it was a woman singing on the road that inspired 'St Louis Blues'. Ma Rainey, along with Bessie Smith and most of the other classic blues singers, also wrote songs, such as 'Bo Weevil Blues', 'Don't Fish in My Sea', 'Louisiana Hoo Doo Blues', 'Prove It on Me Blues', 'Rough and Tumble Blues', 'Titanic Man Blues', 'Weepin' Woman Blues'.

Ma Rainey sang, 'I can't tell you about my future, so I'm going to tell you about my past.' She was on to something even then. If she was around today she would agree with Toni Morrison who said that all the future is in the past. The blueswomen were themselves direct descendants of the Voodoo Queens of the 1800s. As Sally Placksin explains:

Little is known of the earliest queens – Sanité Dédé, Marie Saloppé and the most famous and long-lived queen, Marie Laveau. Free women of color, glamorous and haughty showwomen, shrewd and clever business women, the queens began to accrue power in the early nineteenth century, after the Louisiana Purchase (1803) eased the formerly strict rulings against voodoo in New Orleans . . . After 1817, New Orleans' Place Congo (or Congo Square) was the site where the most public voodoo ceremonies took place. On Sunday afternoons, slaves would gather there to chant and to dance the tamer dances that represented six African tribes . . . Sidney Bechet had grown up hearing about the music played at Congo Square. 'Improvisation', he called it . . . Not only were the voodoo queens and women an important force in the black community . . . the secret voodoo cults also provided an early ground on which women of both races mixed, for some of the women who attended the secret rites were white. Newspaper accounts considered it scandalous when white women were discovered at the ceremonies. (One man actually committed suicide the day after his wife was found at a meeting . . .)[9]

Ma Rainey was the matriarchal head of the original blues family. Every one of the women blues singers must have been influenced by her. Although she did not teach Bessie how to sing (Bessie knew how already; she had a style and a voice of her own), Ma Rainey probably influenced the way that Bessie and the other classic blueswomen dressed, and she almost certainly helped groom Bessie for a life on the road, teaching her dancing steps and the importance of performing her songs, as well as simply singing them. Ma Rainey's grandmother was a stage performer during the Reconstruction. If Ma followed in her grandmother's footsteps, all those classic blues singers who shared the surname of Smith – again as if they were part of the same family – followed in hers. There was Mamie Smith who sang the famous 'Crazy Blues', which, in 1920, was the first commercial classic blues hit. There was Clara Smith, Trixie Smith, Laura Smith and Bessie Smith. They were all unrelated, though often when they were playing together the posters would proclaim, 'The Smith Girls Are in Town'. Sometimes Bessie Smith and Clara Smith – who later recorded 'Far Away Blues' and 'I'm Going Back to My Used to Be' together – pretended to be sisters. The common surname Smith is obviously a legacy of slavery. It created the illusion that large numbers of black people were related because they so frequently shared the surname of their master.

The classic blues singers were not afraid of addressing any issue in their songs. They were far more dynamic in their lyrics than female vocalists today or indeed than any of those singers who followed them. Dinah Washington, Sarah Vaughan, Ella Fitzgerald all sing of milder stuff. The blueswomen sang songs about subjects the Spice Girls would run a mile from (with Sporty Spice in the lead). Sally Placksin again:

> Her subject matter ranged from Everywoman's lovesick, lonesome blues to the havoc wreaked against the men who did her wrong; from anguished desolation to murderous revenge. She counseled women to 'Trust No Man' – not even their own – and advised men to be careful talking in their sleep; she delivered ultimatums, and she dealt frankly and boldly with homosexuality, lesbianism, sadomasochism and sexual violence in her songs.[10]

When they did sing those songs about no-good men, women in the audience would go wild and shout out in agreement. These songs were 'telling it like it is'. They were greeted with such delirious enthusiasm because women identified with the lyrics. Here were songs about ordinary people and ordinary problems. Songs about men, every type of no-count, no-good man it was possible to imagine. A long trail of them, always cheating and letting women down. The classic blues singers sang about life, and ordinary people loved them for it. They sang about illness, death and graveyards as well. No subject was taboo. Memphis Minnie even had a song about meningitis called 'Memphis Minnie-jitis Blues':

Mmmmmmmmm,
The meningitis killing me.
Mmmmmmmmm,
The meningitis killing me.
I'm bending, I'm bending, baby,
My head is nearly down to my knee.

The classic blues singers sang songs that offered wonderful pieces of advice to other women; they were way ahead of their time, giving much more revolutionary advice than today's agony aunts! Ida Cox's 'Wild Women Don't Get the Blues' is exemplary:

You never get nothing by being an angel child,
You better change your ways and get real wild
'Cause wild women don't worry, wild women don't have
    the blues.

There was Bessie, nineteen years old, travelling with the Mother of the Blues. The audience came from miles around; they rode mules or travelled on trains, packed in like rice. The journey to the blues tent must have had nearly as much of a charge of atmosphere as the concert itself.

There they all were, jammed in with other people travelling to hear the same thing, to get the same hit from the blues, coming from all over to experience together the knockout voices of the blueswomen. They came from the river settlements, from cornrows and lumber camps. They travelled miles to get to the hotspot to hear the blues. Sterling Brown captures the mood in his wonderful poem, 'Ma Rainey':

When Ma Rainey
Comes to town
Folks from anyplace
Miles aroun',
From Cape Girardeau,
Poplar Bluff,
Flocks in to hear
Ma do her stuff,
Comes flivverin' in,
Or ridin' mules,
Or packed in trains,
Picknickin' fools . . .
That's what it's like
For miles on down
To New Orleans delta
An' Mobile town,
When Ma hits
Anywheres aroun'.

The tents filled. Even they were segregated – black people on one side and white people on the other. Ma Rainey would come on with greasepaint and powder on her face, wearing an elaborate rhinestone gown, a twenty-dollar gold-piece necklace, flashing those infamous gold and diamond teeth. A mouthful of blues. Ma Rainey's shows went on for two hours. Like the other blues performers, she did not simply sing, she danced and shimmied 'vulgarly'. She was wildly flamboyant and extrovert, a real performer. She got her audiences so worked up and wild that it wasn't so much a call and response as a shout and a shag. Her shows even included acts of freakishness. Ma Rainey loved the double entendres of blues talk; she liked to tease her audiences about bird liver and pig meat. Her repertoire of metaphors for men's sexual anatomy was probably greater than any other blues singer's. Her blues were the lewdest of the lot.

Ma Rainey was also a lesbian. Even though she married Pa Rainey on 22 April 1904, she was still a lesbian. Will Rainey was an older vaudevillean. Together they put on shows and tours for years. It was well known that Ma was a lesbian. Ma and Pa could do just about everything together, touring an act of comedy, singing and dancing, but they couldn't have sex. Amongst the many myths and legends of the Empress are different accounts of Ma Rainey kidnapping Bessie Smith and forcing her to join the Moses Stokes show. Some say she got her henchmen to go down to Charles Street and throw the girl into a big burlap bag to bring her back to her. Others say she carried out the kidnapping herself. At every crucial juncture in Bessie Smith's life there are wild stories, but this is the very best, as Albertson says:

> Legend has it that Ma Rainey literally kidnapped Bessie, that she and her husband forced the girl to tour with their show, teaching her in the process how to sing the blues. It's a colorful story, but almost certainly just a story. 'I remember one time when we were in Augusta, Georgia,' says Maud Smith [wife of Bessie's brother Clarence]. 'Bessie and Ma Rainey sat down and had a good laugh about how people was making up stories of Ma taking Bessie from her home, and Ma's mother used to get the biggest laugh out of the kidnapping story whenever we visited her in Macon. Actually, Ma and Bessie got along fine, but Ma never taught Bessie how to sing. She was more like a mother to her.[11]

The person who first made up this story would never have thought of a motive. Why would Ma Rainey have wanted to do it? Maybe the story came about because of Ma Rainey's renowned lesbianism. Maybe the gossips thought it figured a girl like Ma Rainey would need a companion. Perhaps it is all down to the notion, the prejudice, that lesbians coerce, force, mislead, kidnap, rather than fall in love. But it is still a good story. Years later, whenever Ma Rainey and Bessie Smith met up, they had a good laugh about it.

*There would have been no ransom, that's for sure. No note except a blue note. A getaway wagon, not a getaway car. And the hideout was the Moses Stokes Travelling Show. The Moses Stokes Travelling Show. How high the stake? How much did Ma Rainey want Bessie Smith to sing the blues? Would she have given her life?*

*It happens in the dead of night with Bessie asleep in the middle of Viola and Tinnie. Ma Rainey arrives in the wagon with Pa. Ma Rainey is so bored of Pa. Pa never even tries to get it on with her. The names Ma and Pa are so asexual. It is never possible to imagine a wildly passionate relationship between a Ma and a Pa. (It is the same with the Broons. Ma and Pa Broon have heaps of kids but you can never imagine how they got them.) Pa Rainey knows he is a laughing stock but something about those gold teeth of Ma's makes him do whatever she says. A man can be ruled by a woman with gold teeth. He knows his wife wants this young girl Bessie Smith and there ain't a single thing he can do about it. He aids and abets her. He waits outside, smoking a pipe, whilst Ma is inside kidnapping. It is not for nothing that Ma and Pa are called the Assassinators of the Blues. They take the role very seriously. Before coming tonight for the young Bessie Smith, they have both intoxicated themselves with hashish. Pa has to help Ma on with the stocking. It is one from the current show. He pulls it over her face. Its purpose is to disguise those gold teeth. Ma Rainey's teeth are the most famous teeth in the whole of America. Even with*

*the stocking on, Pa glimpses a frightening flash of gold.
He tells his wife to shut her mouth, to do the deed with no
words. Then he lights up his pipe again. Ma Rainey will
not bungle it. She wants the girl too bad. The things she's
heard about this girl. Skin saw her on the corner of Ninth
Street just last week singing like her soul was on fire. Skin
told Ma how he had stood transfixed on the spot for four
hours, how he hadn't even noticed the rain coming down,
how he only moved when he suddenly realised the girl had
gone. Ma had pulled his collar and said, 'Where did she
go?' But the useless pig meat knew nothing. Ma had to
assign somebody else to track down that girl's cabin. A girl
that could sing like that was worth having. Ma Rainey
opens the door quietly and picks up the girl in the middle in
her arms. Tinnie and Viola don't even turn in their sleep or
grind their teeth some more. Nothing. And this Bessie she's
heard so much about weighs some but Ma's arms are strong
as a lesbian's. Her feet don't exactly manage a straight
path to the cabin's door, but this singing girl is sleeping like
a log. Ma wants to kiss her beautiful black sleeping face,
those nice peachy lips she has, but she stops herself. There
will be time enough for all that when she gets her back to
Moses Stokes. She'll need to make sure no one else gets to
her first though. This blues girl will be worth it. Worth it
when she teaches her those shouts. She is going to teach that
girl to sing the blues in the morning – and come night-time
that girl will be singing the blues like she been singing them
all her life. Her voice will make her want her all the more.*

51

*And when they are both finished with Rabbit's Foot and
Cotton Blossoms, Ma Rainey will devour her. She will get
her going till she don't know where she's heading for.*

Everyone knew that Ma was a lesbian. Ma even sang songs
with overtly lesbian themes:

I went out last night with a crowd of my friends
It must have been womens 'cause I don't like no men.

'Prove It on Me'

Maybe Ma being so open about her sexuality encouraged
Bessie to do likewise. Bessie was never hung up about her
relationships with women; neither was Ma. I like to picture
the pair of them on the wagon on the road, laughing and
giggling at some foolish remark some foolish man just said.
I like to see Ma's mouth wide and grinning, flashing bits of
gold. There's the dust on the road, and the road is bumpy
and travelling isn't always fun. But sometimes the journey would pass quick with Ma and Bessie gossiping and
making up blues together. Bessie was a novice. Her brother
Clarence had suddenly changed her life. One moment she
was singing on Ninth Street, the next she was off with Ma
and Pa Rainey, the Assassinators of the Blues, on the road,
travelling through the South and the Midwest.

Bessie Smith is now known as a blues singer. But in the
days when she performed live, she was multi-talented and
versatile. Her dancing was as good as her singing. She liked

acting too, dressing up in various costumes. She appeared as a singer, dancer and male impersonator in her own show, *Liberty Belles Revue*, at the 91 Theatre, Atlanta, 1918–19. (I bet she made a handsome man.) She worked with the Charley Taylor Band in local clubs in Atlantic City and she was in New Jersey in the early 1920s with the Charles Johnson Band in Paradise Gardens. She worked in Horan's Madhouse Club in Philadelphia from 1920 to 1923. She appeared with Sidney Bechet in the musical comedy show *How Come* at the Dunbar Theatre in 1923. Sidney Bechet has turned out to be one of the most perceptive commentators about Bessie Smith. He claimed to have had a love affair with her. Whether he did or not is unproven, but he certainly, early on, managed to grasp her complexity:

> She had this trouble in her, this thing that would not let her rest sometimes, a meanness that came and took her over. But what she had was alive . . . Bessie, she just wouldn't let herself be; it seemed she couldn't let herself be.[12]

Having travelled with so many troupes, she already had a large following before she made her first record. Her experiences on the road were forming the tough and uncompromising woman she was to become. She had so many encounters with racism, from black people as well as white, who thought her skin colour was just too dark, that it is easy to see how she developed a toughness to survive.

Doing the clubs, Bessie eventually became so successful and had such an enthusiastic following that she could insist on being the only one on the bill who would sing the blues. She came to regard the blues as her territory. She said to Ethel Waters (who she called 'Long Goody'):

You ain't so bad. It's only I never dreamed that anyone would be able to do this to me in my own territory and with my own people. And you know damn well that you can't sing worth a ——— [13]

The Empress was a prima donna. But then she had that voice, that talent. She could cast a spell on her audience. She could hypnotise them. She had them under her blues.

Picture her: 1921, 1922, bigger now, older now, wearing fancy clothes. She's made big money; she's drunk bootleg; she's had sex with women and men. But the little girl's face is still just behind the woman's. Pentimento. When she gets up to shout the blues, to barrelhouse, to transform her audience, part of her is still standing on Ninth Street under the moody sky. The part of her that is still standing on Ninth Street is the part of her that hypnotises the audience in the 81 Club in Atlanta, Georgia. This power she has, she was born with. It is nothing new to her. It is not really a surprise. She was just waiting for it to find a bigger place than a street corner and it did. It found a dress, a dress she thought would do. She wasn't really all that bothered about what she wore anyhow. (Except for the shoes. The leather always felt important on her feet after all those years of being barefooted.) She felt fat and clumsy in every damn dress whether it was cotton, linen or kiss-her-black-ass silk. It found a club, then it would find, in a few years, a record, then it would break the record. She wears fancy dresses now on the stage, after Ma Rainey. Ma Rainey's flamboyance set the trend for the blueswomen. I've never seen a photograph of a woman singing the blues in a wee grey slip.

When Bessie sings in these clubs with the audience literally spellbound, captivated, totally enthralled, she is not really paying them any attention. She is deep, deep inside herself in the place where the blues come from. She has shut out the clapping and the stomping and the shouting. It is quiet in the 81 Club, people's faces are like stills. They flash before her sometimes in the middle of a song. Like something she might see travelling on a train very fast; seen for an instant then gone. She catches the odd glimpses of one shining face and another troubled one and then she returns to herself. Sometimes she's sure she saw her sister Tinnie right in the middle of that sea of faces in the 81 Club. Once she even saw her dead mother standing for a single moment behind the bar. After singing the blues, she knocks down one drink, then another, full of a terrible longing for herself, for her family, for Chattanooga. The whole theatre is full of a restless longing. She gets people that way. She is right under their skin. She is closer than God.

She hasn't made a record yet. But she has tapped the source of her own power – her voice – and she knows it is like nobody else's and she doesn't want the distraction of anybody else playing with the blues. No, she is the blues. She is the blues itself. As far as she is concerned, she is the rightful Queen of the Blues and nobody else can sing worth a damn. She knows the timing. She's got the timing just right. Doesn't need to articulate it or even to think about it. It's all in the length of her pause. It's the way she hangs on to those notes when they are gone. Like she's hanging on to the little girl she was, or the very back of herself, or her grandmother's long, large hand. She is full of longing, full of trouble, restless, wandering up and down the long arms of the clock. When she sings on stage, part of her is travelling, reaching back into every hurt that's ever happened. Her voice is a poplar tree singing. Swaying in the Southern breeze.

Who knows better than we,
With the dark, dark bodies,
What it means
When April comes alaughing and aweeping
Once again
At our hearts?
                    Angelina Weld Grimké, 'At April'

# THE TRUNK AND THE NO-GOOD MAN

Bessie Smith married twice. The marriage to her first husband, Earl Love, lasted only one year before he died. Nothing is known about Earl Love except that he came from a prominent black Mississippi family. In 1922 Bessie Smith met Jack Gee. On 7 June 1923 he obtained their marriage licence from the clerk at the Orphans' Court, Philadelphia County. They then went on to the house of a Reverend C. A. Tindley, a prolific composer of gospel songs, the most famous of which was 'We Shall Overcome', and Jack Gee and Bessie Smith were pronounced man and wife. But Bessie never became Bessie Gee. Throughout her career, she was known as Bessie Smith.

Their relationship lasted six years and obsessed Bessie for several more. The key to understanding Bessie Smith lies in understanding the pull and power that men like Jack had. Jack was a big strong man who had no special talents or skills of his own. He loved power and from the outset of his relationship with Bessie he tried to take over her life and control her. Her wild excessive drinking drove him crazy and he often beat her up for getting drunk. Being a famous blues star did not stop Bessie from being a battered wife. Jack frequently beat her up very badly, knocking her downstairs and threatening to kill her. The few people on the road who went to her defence were beaten up too.

Jack would beat up any chorine who got between him and Bessie. When she travelled with her performing girls and prop boys and her band, everyone was terrified of Jack's sudden appearances.

Jack Gee was a nightwatchman, an illiterate, who had been turned down by the Philadelphia Police Department; yet he often pretended that he was a policeman. Bessie's Smith husband, a policeman? The image of her in feathers, plumes and ermine coat, and him in his imaginary police-man's uniform, arresting people at her gigs, is hilarious. The joke was on Jack; he couldn't see it. If he had been a real policeman he probably would even have enjoyed arresting his drunken wife to thwart her devilish drinking. He would have relished throwing her in a cell and telling her to stay there till morning. Jack could only fantasise. He never made the grade. Why did Jack want to be a policeman anyway? He wanted to have the legal power to intimidate people and excuse his excesses in the name of the law. He wanted a uniform. He wanted respect from the wearing of the uni-form. He wanted everyone to obey his every command. He didn't get to join the Philadelphia Police Department but he did a good job of being that impromptu self-appointed cop on the road. Bessie Smith's fame gave him a vicarious power which he used unsparingly.

Apparently, Jack Gee's favourite pastime was counting Bessie Smith's money. He was good at counting. He loved it. He would often stay up until the wee small hours sep-arating nickels from dimes, quarters from halves. Every tiny coin counted. Although Bessie disapproved of his money-counting binges, she found them amusing. She often entertained her friends mimicking the big-eyed Jack, crouched over and stroking tiny towers of change.

Bessie met Jack in 1922, when she was appearing in Philadelphia at Horah's Cabaret before she made her first record, but well after she had made a big name for herself on the road. Bessie Smith's life is so full of drama, it seems really over the top. Her life was theatre. It is impossible to separate Bessie's blues from Bessie. She is her blues. 'She was blues from the time she got up in the morning until she went to bed at night,' Frank Walker – who later became her manager – asserted.[14]

On her very first date with Jack somebody shot him and nearly killed him. (Wasn't that enough of a sign for her?) So, on her first date, she is not stood up, or given a dizzy, as we used to say in Glasgow, but her date is shot. *Her date is shot.* You can't fuck a man with a bullet through him, but you can visit him in hospital and tend to his wounds. Bessie visited Jack daily for five weeks and became close to him. (Closer probably than if they had fucked that first night.) The strange intimacy that comes from hospital visits, the complicit vulnerability, the knowledge of the daily routine, the familiarity of every need, would have given Bessie a false sense of Jack's character. She would have been moved by his need for her. His violence would have been checked under those hospital sheets.

When he came out of hospital, Bessie already had her

first recording date for 'Downhearted Blues'. He pawned his watch so that he could buy her a red dress for the occasion. A gift that she never forgot. It was probably the single thing that tied her to him for all those years. Nobody had ever bought her anything before. No man had ever pawned his watch for her before. She took the dress as a sign of love. She loved the dress. When she sang that first song wearing the red dress that Jack bought, she probably felt lucky. Who knows, if she was superstitious (which she was apparently), she might have felt she owed her entire recording career to that one dress. Ludicrous as it may seem, there must be something that explains his enormous hold over her. There she was, an independent woman who had wealth, fame and success, tied to a man who was beating her up and trying to control her life. Did she believe he loved her because he pawned his watch? Did she love him because he pawned his watch? What was it about Jack Gee that made Bessie stick with him for so long? She was not faithful to him, but she was obsessed with him. She did everything to try and make him happy. After she started making lots of money with her recordings, he gave up his job as nightwatchman. She bought him a good gold watch. (Maybe that's why he pawned that watch; he knew she'd buy him a better one.) She bought him expensive cars if he so much as looked in their direction. She sent him off frequently to Hot Springs when he was having his 'breakdowns'. She even wrote a song about Hot Springs.

Some come here crippled, some come here lame
If they don't go away well, we are not to blame
Hot spring water sure runs good and hot.


According to Maud Smith, Bessie's sister-in-law: 'Jack never had no nervous breakdowns. . . We were the ones who should have had nervous breakdowns. He wasn't sick. Bessie would do anything for him, so she'd give him all the money he wanted, and tell him to go and take a rest.'[15] Perhaps being ill, or pretending to be ill, was also a way of controlling Bessie. If he couldn't stop her wild partying ways by beating her up, he could go to Hot Springs and make her visit him. Perhaps he wanted her to feel guilty at the state he was in. Or maybe it reminded him of their wooing when he was in hospital recovering from the gunshot.

Jack Gee applied for a marriage licence as 'Downhearted Blues' hit the market. Irony rarely comes so rich:

Gee, but it's hard to love someone, when that someone
    don't love you.
I'm so disgusted, heartbroken too, I've got those
    downhearted blues.
Once I was crazy about a man, he mistreated me all the
    time.
The next man I get has got to promise me to be mine all
    mine.
Trouble, trouble, I've had it all my days,

Trouble, trouble, I've had it all my days,
It seems like trouble is going to follow me to my grave.

This song was prophetic; no need for a glass ball when you've got the blues. At this point the marriage with Jack was reasonably happy, full of the promise of the future. But the real future of 'Downhearted Blues' was lying in wait and it wasn't long before Jack started mistreating Bessie. Once begun, the cycle of destructiveness seemed unbreakable. The relationship was always on the brink of crisis. They were always breaking up and making up. They were addicted to each other even though they must have known they were bad for each other and totally incompatible. Bessie was a big drinker; Jack was teetotal. Bessie was wildly sociable; Jack was antisocial. Bessie liked wild parties; Jack hated them. Bessie was generous with her money; Jack was mean. Bessie was talented; Jack was not. What did they have in common? Singing the blues on the road became a vital means of escape from the tyrannical Jack. But she couldn't stop him popping up all the time. Jack Gee cramped her style. She could not enjoy partying, drink or promiscuous sex with him around. It is strange that she married him in the first place; home life never did seem to make her very happy. She did not even spend much time or money making a nice home for them. They had an apartment at 1236 Webster Street in Philadelphia, but it lacked the atmosphere of a home. There was no fancy furniture. 'There was nothing special about it,' said Ruby Walker, Jack's niece.[16]

The majority of Bessie Smith's blues concern that 'dog-gone man of mine'. Although they were not all written by Bessie, they could easily all have been about one man: Jack Gee. The famous lines, 'I've got the world in a jug, The stopper's in my hand', at the end of 'Downhearted Blues' are still powerful. The mixture of enigma and plain talking is typical blues. What do they mean? Are they positive or negative or both? Those lines were so popular because people identified with them. People would sing those lines to themselves as if they aptly captured some truth about their own life. All the conflicts, wars and sorrows, the pains and the troubles of the world are in Bessie's jug, but the stopper's in her hand. She has some power over it then. Or is she just singing about the world of men, the world of mistreating men? And has she cast herself in the role of Everywoman? The world's experiences contain her own; she is the woman in the street who can never get away from man trouble – it will follow her to her grave. But she has that stopper in her hand. Maybe it is men she can put a stop to if she wants to, a stop to all that heartbreak. Maybe all the lying, cheating, dirty no-gooders are in that jug. A blues song, like a poem, opens itself up to multiple interpretations. There's the words and there's the music contradicting the words, adding irony and changing the meaning.

Jack tried to control Bessie's affairs but he never was her business manager. Maud Smith said in conversation with Chris Albertson, scathingly, some years later:

Jack couldn't even manage himself. He would always have signs saying, 'Jack Gee presents Bessie Smith' and he would call himself a manager, but he couldn't even sell a ticket. He could count money and he could ask for money, but that's about it.[17]

So why did Bessie Smith, the Empress, the Queen of the Blues, waste her time and much of her life with a living example of the dirty no-gooders she sang about? On the one hand, there's this strong woman who would fight anyone who said one wrong word, who stood up for herself and others, who refused to be patronised by white people or intimidated by club owners, managers or recording companies; on the other, there's this battered wife who lived in fear of her husband discovering any of her wild parties, who kept him on, despite the numerous times he beat her up, who was so frightened of him she was unable to get rid of him. In the end, Jack Gee broke Bessie down so much that her friends and family could hardly recognise her. A dancer in the Moaning Low Company said, 'She wouldn't cry, she'd just sit there, staring . . . sometimes I just couldn't believe that this was the same woman. That man really broke her down, strong as she was.'[18]

Bessie never recovered from his affair with Gertrude Saunders, Irving C. Miller's most glorious 'brownskin beauty'. (There is a bitter irony here since it was Miller who years before had turned Bessie down for being 'too dark'.) Gertrude Saunders was well known in Miller's

1926 show, *Red Hot Mama*. She was also famous for her performances in *Liza* and *Shuffle Along*. In 1929, six years after their marriage and 'Downhearted Blues', Jack used Bessie Smith's money to finance Gertrude Saunders in her own show, then on tour in Columbus, Ohio. Bessie found out because a man turned up at her show, *Steamboat Days*, and showed her a copy of an article in the *Amsterdam News* which recounted Jack's considerable success with the Gertrude Saunders show. True to form, Bessie was off like a shot, hiring a cab all the way to Columbus, accompanied by her constant companion, Ruby Walker. She tracked down his hotel in thirty minutes and went to have a piece of him. The hotel room was a shambles. There was blood, guts, pieces of furniture and feathers flying everywhere. 'Downhearted Blues' came into being for real – *Once I was crazy about a man, he mistreated me all the time.* This wasn't a blues song. This was real life. Question: what is the difference between the blues and real life? Answer: truth is stranger than the blues.

Nobody knows when Jack began his relationship with Gertrude Saunders; and Gertrude Saunders herself denied they ever had a relationship at all, claiming that Jack was 'just an ignorant darkie, but he had a good business head on him, and he was perfect for Bessie; those two belonged together.'[19] It is certain that the marriage to Jack ended in that hotel room. It was never the same afterwards. So Jack moved on to the Gertrude Saunders show, moving out of Bessie's life. Bessie Smith's adopted son, Jack Junior, claims that Gertrude did have a relationship with Jack Gee senior. According to him, Jack even brought Gertrude round to Bessie's house when she was away on the road. But Jack Gee's biggest betrayal of Bessie Smith concerned not Gertrude Saunders, but Jack Junior.

It was while she was on tour that Bessie first met her adopted son-to-be. Every time she went through Macon, Georgia, she would stop to spend time with the boy she called 'Snooks'. His mother was a niece of Margaret Warren, one of Bessie Smith's chorus girls. She had promised Bessie that if she ever ran into trouble she would let Bessie adopt her son. In the spring of 1926 Jack Gee and Bessie legally adopted Snooks, renaming him Jack Gee Junior. He was six years old when he was brought to Philadelphia on Bessie's railroad car. He joined them on the last round of that tour. Bessie Smith was overjoyed to have this son in her life. She resolved to cut out her drinking and try and create a stable family home for him. She sent for her family, who were still living in Chattanooga, so that they could help her with him when she was on tour. She bought two houses close together, 1143 and 1147 Kater Street. One was for Viola and her family and the other for Lulu and Tinnie and their families. At this period in her life, she was at her happiest. She had her family up from Chattanooga. She had enough money to buy them houses. She had a son. She showered everybody with gifts. Having a son to look after gave her a real purpose in life and she took it very seriously. She wanted him to get a good education, said she would buy him anything if he became a lawyer. Having Jack Junior gave Bessie Smith another identity. She was proud of being a mother.

Perhaps out of a desire to get revenge on Bessie, or perhaps just to make his destructive impact on her life long-lasting, Jack Gee ensured that Bessie lost not just him but their son. After leaving Bessie, he kidnapped Jack Junior and put him into care. He had no real interest in his name-sake but he knew how much the boy meant to Bessie. Jack Junior, tracked down by Chris Albertson, tells the story:

> One day when Mama wasn't home and he was living with Gertrude [Saunders] at her house, he came and got me. He told me to get in the car and said that he wanted to take me somewhere. So I got in the car and wound up at the SPCC (Society for Prevention of Cruelty to Children). They kept me down there for about two weeks – he told the people that Mama let me stay out all night, which was a lie.[20]

Jack Junior escaped from the SPCC only to find himself back with his father, whose partner made him sleep in the basement with her brother. The brother got him up the next morning and made him clean the hall. It must have been such a shock for Jack Junior to go from living with Bessie Smith for five years as her pride and joy, with a more than comfortable lifestyle, to cleaning the hall in the basement of a strange house at the age of eleven. After Bessie's death in 1937, Jack Gee Senior took all of her money, claiming that they still had a close relationship. Her son, who should have inherited the lot, was left poor. Jack Gee made sure he was never mentioned and that no writer knew of his existence. It wasn't until Chris Albertson's book came out in 1971 that the rest of the world knew of his existence.

The blues that Bessie sang often strangely anticipated her life. She became her blues. Or perhaps she always was her blues. So many of the tragedies she sang about actually happened to her after she sang the songs and not before; she didn't just sing songs that reflected her own experience, she sang songs about experiences that were lying in wait for her, further on down that old blues road. Her blues were premonitions. Some of them she wrote herself, but the majority were written by other people. It is not clear how much freedom she had in choosing her songs. But it is surely no coincidence that the next song she recorded after her devastating break-up with Jack was the quintessential 'Nobody Knows You When You're Down and Out', written by Jimmy Cox.

This song, more than any other, is the song that most people associate with Bessie Smith and it remains tremendously popular. She recorded it on 15 May 1929, accompanied by an accomplished five-piece band, and Columbia released it on 13 September. When she sang, 'Then I began to fall so low, / I didn't have a friend and no place to go, . . . It's mighty strange, without a doubt / Nobody knows you when you're down and out,' the truth of those words resonated throughout the North and the South. She hummed half the song, a haunting solo by trumpeter Ed Allen, 'Mmmmmmmmmmmmmmm when you're down and out', expressing the feeling of it even more movingly than words could do. Jack was gone in May of the same year. Her loss comes through; what other song at this point in her life could possibly have put it better? Or worse – since the pain in her voice is almost unbearable? And it prophesied Bessie's future. She was once a woman who gave everything to friends and family, buying them houses and expensive gifts. But when she fell so low, there was hardly a soul to help her, except Richard Morgan (her lover for the last six years of her life, but he comes later). Even her own sisters, when she started making less money in the late 1920s and early 1930s, resented the drop in their allowance and barely spoke to her. Everyone had grown to depend on her making big money, so much so that they almost despised her for not pulling it in any more. No wonder the last lines are so resonant:

So if I ever get my hands on a dollar again
I'm going to hold on to it 'til them eagles grin.

Bessie Smith's life, as a poor girl in a ramshackle cabin, to Queen of the Blues, to the fallen betrayed queen of a dying music, has Shakespearean dimensions, a shattering combination of tragedy and comedy. Jack Gee's betrayal of Bessie signalled the very beginning of the downward spiral; not long afterwards, the blues themselves became victims of the Wall Street Crash and were almost killed by the Depression. Bessie experienced its effects firsthand. Theatres closed down; others replaced their stage shows with talking pictures. People didn't have the same kind of money to buy blues records. Columbia terminated her contract in 1931, two years after the Crash. People still turned out to hear her, from Mobile, Alabama, to New Orleans to Dallas. But a concession Bessie had to make during these years was to share the bill with other blues singers, whose talents didn't match hers and whose fame did not last as hers has. A couple of years after the Crash, even live audiences were sorely affected. People queued for bread, not blues. Money was tight, and for those who could afford it the blues started to go out of fashion, to be replaced by jazz. The tastes of the Northern audiences changed dramatically: they wanted faster, more sophisticated voices, voices that could swing. All the downhome people who had found in the blues a cure for homesickness were now firmly rooted in the North and ready to move on in their cultural tastes. The bottom fell out of the blues recording industry.

Bessie Smith's voice could and did swing; it is one of the greatest jazz – not just blues – voices of the twentieth century. With her penchant for timing and her way of dipping down notes and hanging on to others, she almost certainly would have survived the Depression and gone on to sing standard jazz songs. Her style of dragging over a word or syllable into the next bar was copied by many others. Her genius for timing set the trend for jazz singers for generations. She knew how to hang up a note and when to let it down. Humphrey Lyttelton is convinced her recording of 'Nobody Knows You' 'stamps Bessie Smith as a supreme jazz singer':

> This is the standard which Bessie Smith set for all jazz singers to follow, using improvisation in its fullest sense on the melody of a song to express a deeper meaning than that of the words on their own. It was an example which, a decade later, enabled Billie Holiday to make remarkable music out of the popular ditties of the calibre of 'I Cried for You' and 'Back in Your Own Back Yard', not to mention 'Oooooooh, What a Little Moonlight Can Do'.[21]

But back then, she was known of and thought of as a blues singer. In the 1930s a new generation of jazz women came to the fore: Billie Holiday, Mildred Bailey, Ella Fitzgerald, Connee Boswell. So Bessie Smith lost her man and lost her power to earn really big bucks almost simultaneously. She was broken by Jack's betrayal, lost a lot of her fighting spunk and was often seen crying. (Ruby had never seen her cry before.) Bessie recorded 'Shipwreck Blues' in late 1931, although it wasn't released until July 1932. Columbia only ordered four hundred copies to be made – a far cry from the 780,000 copies of 'Downhearted Blues' sold in its first six months, making the fate of 'Shipwreck Blues' doubly ironic.

It's rainin' and it's stormin'
On the sea,
It's rainin' and it's stormin'
On the sea,
I feel like somebody has shipwrecked poor me.

Not only did Bessie lose her man – something she had sung about so often in her recording career – but she lost him to a 'glorious brownskin' girl. 'Downhearted Blues' should have served as a warning: 'It seems like trouble is going to follow me to my grave.' Jack Gee did break her heart; she never really recovered from his betrayal. Only for the first couple of years of their marriage was she happy, although fanatically busy recording songs and going on tour. (She was so happy because she was away from him so much and the thought of him and having a husband at home was much better than the reality. The actual homecoming and the wearing of the housecoat and slippers was a disappointment.)

Jack Gee didn't just play a destructive role in Bessie Smith's life; he played a destructive role in her afterlife. His greed for her money has had a long-lasting and devastating effect on the way in which we remember Bessie Smith, from his refusal to give over the money raised at benefits to buy her a gravestone, to his refusal to co-operate with a potential biographer, as recorded by Chris Albertson:

Jazz critic Rudi Blesh has recalled how close he
came to writing a Bessie Smith biography in the
late nineteen-forties, when the available sources
of information were more numerous. Bessie's
sisters, Tinnie and Viola – then still alive, living in
Philadelphia – had agreed, along with Jack Gee, to
co-operate in piecing together Bessie's life. The two
sisters had a trunk full of rare photographs, letters,
sheet music, and other items that had belonged to
Bessie . . . Just as the work was to begin, Jack Gee
decided he wanted more money. His unrealistic
demand made the project impossible, reignited his
long-running feud with the two sisters, caused them to
withdraw, and led to the complete disappearance of the
trunk and its valuable contents.[22]

This is the kind of story that makes biographers weep.
A whole trunk of stuff. It's shattering to imagine all the
information that would have been available had the trunk
been handed over. Jack almost certainly was threatened by
his wife's success. Why else hijack the biography? Why
did Jack prevent that book? Was it just greed, or could
he not bear the story of Bessie Smith being told? Did he
consciously or subconsciously stop that book from being
written? The policeman in him got rid of the evidence.
What was in that trunk?

*Before they died, Tinnie and Viola sent it on a ship heading for Scotland. They had seen pictures of Scotland and liked the look of the country, those big goddam mountains. Could send Jack up one of those and he'd never come down. Ben Nevis. They didn't want Jack to get his hands on that trunk, ever. He was a dirty no-gooder and Bessie should have known better. She ought never have married the skunk. A note to this effect is found sixty years later, signed by both of them. Tinnie's writing is perfect calligraphy and Viola's is big childish print.*

*Inside: an old photograph of the shack in Chattanooga where Bessie was born. Nobody is standing outside it. It is just the shack. It is dark and leaning to the left. The window is partly boarded up. The door is flung open like somebody just left in a hurry. It's been taken on a bright day. The bright sunlight has blanched out some bits of the roof.*

*An early daguerreotype of Bessie Smith's mother and her father. She favours her mother, got her nose and her chin and especially her eyes. But she has inherited the shape of her father's face. Her mother and father are standing side by side, and the electricity between them is still there in the image.*

*An old poster advertising the two Assassinators of the Blues in the Moses Stokes Travelling Show, yellow and curled at the edges.*

*Another picture, of Bessie herself standing on the corner of Ninth Street singing.*

*A baby tooth, next to a wisdom tooth, which has its long roots still, also attached, wrapped in newspaper.*

*A bottle of bootleg liquor and a pint glass with a lipstick imprint of the lips of the Empress. A horsehair wig – shiny black hair that once long ago ran all the way down to the round shoulders of Bessie Smith. A strand of pearls and imitation rubies. A satin dress. Headgear that looks like a lampshade in someone's front room with lots of tassels hanging down. A plain dress with beaded fringes. A Spanish shawl. A skullcap with beads and pearls sewn into it. Feathers. Ostrich plumes. An ermine coat. A giant bottle of Coca-Cola.*

*A notebook in Bessie's handwriting of all her own blues compositions.*

*A letter full of curses, again in Bessie's handwriting, to the manager of the 91 Club in Atlanta. An original record of 'Downhearted Blues'. A reject selection of the songs that were never released. A giant pot of chicken stew still steaming, its lid tilted to the side. A photograph of Ethel Waters; underneath the sophisticated image Bessie has written: 'Northern bitch. Long goody. Sweet Mama Stringbean. 1922'. A photograph of Ruby. Bessie has written all over her face words that are impossible to decipher. Another photograph of Ruby, untouched, in a sexy pose and wearing a polka-dot dress with separate sleeves and a string of pearls. A jar of Harlem night air.*

*A blues for Ruby. A blues so raunchy it will become a lesbian classic. Every lesbian singer will make a recording of it. Sometime in the future, technology will be so sophisticated, a recording will be made of Bessie*

Smith singing 'Ruby's Blues'; they will have succeeded in cutting a whole new blues by piecing together words from her previous songs and connecting them digitally. Bessie's version will outsell anyone else's, including k. d. lang.

A conical horn. A diary of the road, written by Bessie. Contains much hot gossip and many lavish curses. Every player gets a mention. Clarence Williams has more swear words attributed to him than anyone else, except Jack Gee, because he stole Bessie's money too. There are foul nicknames too rude to quote here for Carl Van Vechten, Gertrude Saunders, Jack Gee, Frank Walker, Clarence Williams and brownskin girls everywhere. All the clubs have code names. The 81 is nicknamed 'The Black Ass Club'. A long list of every woman Bessie Smith ever had sex with. A list of all the women Ma Rainey had sex with.

An old street map of Goose Hollow with faded pencil drawings of all three stores. A cross by Bessie's cabin.

A photograph of Snooks, taken in Macon, Georgia, in 1925. Another picture of him a year later, getting onto Bessie's railroad car. Bessie's written 'My son' on it.

A pillow from Bessie Smith's bed with her smell still on it. The dress she wore for the recording of 'Nobody Knows You When You're Down and Out' with her odour round the rim of the oxters. A photograph of the Smiths when Bessie was four. Andrew's top two teeth missing. Viola long and skinny. Tinnie holding Bessie's hand. Clarence looking serious. Maud holding her stomach laughing. One of them is missing.

*At the bottom of the missing trunk is something that is very old and shrivelled up. It is a pig's foot. The pigfoot is swimming in water. It is the Tennessee River. A backdrop of a bright full moon floats on the river along with sheets of blues music that have been made into tiny boats. The music of Clarence Williams, Fletcher Henderson, Buster Bailey, Coleman Hawkins, Joe Smith, Louis Armstrong. The original sheets of music inside the missing trunk, folded into tiny boats and floating on the brown water of the Tennessee. The backdrop she always used, magnolia trees, in silhouette set against an orange sky, floats on the saltless water of the Tennessee. Andrew's guitar rows itself down the water. A couple of shipwrecked blues musicians sit inside it, pulling the strings apart to keep their heads above water. The voice of the young girl on the corner recorded at the very beginning of wax recordings. Somebody took her into a strange barn where she had to sing, 'Swing Low, Sweet Chariot, Papa's going to carry you home,' into an odd object that looked like an animal's horn.*

*Her Bible with the exact date of her birth: 15 April 1894. A marriage certificate with the date of her birth – 1894, Chattanooga. A legal certificate of adoption, naming Bessie Smith as Jack Gee Junior's mother. A divorce certificate dated 19 October 1931.*

*Her death certificate: 26 September 1937. Obituaries from the* Boston Globe *and the* New York Times *and the* St Louis Record. *The steering wheel of the $5,000 Cadillac she bought Jack. A letter from the hospital where*

*Bessie Smith died, claiming to have treated her straight away, signed by Dr W. H. Brandon, M.D.*

*A piece of Route 61. Her bed from her Pullman. A tiny Pullman porter in his uniform, perfectly preserved. Ma Rainey's gold fillings.*

*A lock of Ruby's thick black hair.*

Pour O pour that parting soul in song,
O pour it in the sawdust glow of night,
Into the velvet pine-smoke air to-night,
And let the valley carry it along.
And let the valley carry it along.

Jean Toomer, 'Song of the Son'


She came out on the stage in ostrich feathers, beaded
  satin,
and shone that smile on us and didn't need the lights
  and sang.

Robert E. Hayden, 'Homage to the<br>Empress of the Blues'

# WAX

Why the blues are part of me – almost religious, like a chant. The blues are like spirituals, almost sacred. When we sing the blues, we're singing out our hearts . . . our feelings.

Alberta Hunter

The fact that we ever got to hear any of the classic blues singers at all is a total historical accident. Mamie Smith was the first to record a blues song, 'Crazy Blues'. The Okeh Record Company were trying to find Sophie Tucker to record some songs. Her voice was mellow and she was white, but they couldn't contact her, so they decided to take a risk with Mamie Smith, a black vaudeville singer who didn't have half of Bessie's on-the-road followers. The first record Mamie Smith made with the Okeh label was not a blues. But for the second, her gutsy manager, Perry Bradford, persuaded the Okeh company to let her sing the blues backed by a black band. The result was 'Crazy Blues', which was cut on 10 August 1920. It was a huge hit, selling over a hundred thousand copies during the first month of its release. Little business sat up and wanted to be big business.

The blueswomen had taken the blues from backrooms in backstreets first onto the stage, and now onto the record.

The blues were changed by the blueswomen, no longer a folk music sung by folk in the fields, calling and responding to one another while they worked, or while the sun set, folk who wore poor country suits that hadn't been made for them, or vests with holes in them. We have all seen the pictures. In fact, the picture has come back recently in stereotyped romanticisation of the old bluesmen. Now they are being used to sell beer in television and cinema ads, sitting on that sepia porch with the bad-fitting brown suits to sell a bottle of beer. These old bluesmen are considered the genuine article while the women are fancy dress. The poorer the bluesman looks on that run-down porch, the more authentic his blues. The image of the blueswomen is the exact opposite of the bluesmen. There they are in all their splendour and finery, their feathers and ostrich plumes and pearls, theatrical smiles, theatrical shawls, dressed up to the nines and singing about the jail house. The blueswomen are never seen wearing white vests or poor dresses, sitting on a porch in some small Southern town. No, they are right out there on that big stage, prima donnas, barrelhousing, shouting, strutting their stuff. They are all theatre. This combination of theatre and truth is at the heart of the blueswomen. They might be dressed up as divas, queens and empresses, but they are still telling it like it is. The audience never doubts the truth of the humour or the truth of the sadness, as Sally Placksin writes:

Women shouted recognition when the singer told about the way her man mistreated her, they shouted confirmation when Bessie Smith sang her 'Young Woman's Blues' or when Ma Rainey majestically dumped her man in 'Titanic Man Blues'. Some nights the shouts turned into silence as the congregations sat spellbound in the mystical presence of Ma Rainey or 'Miss Bessie.' Like all artists, musicians, actors and show people in those years, the blues women were considered by many, even in the black community, the 'lowest of the low'.[23]

It is all there in the blues: believable and fanciful at the same time. The opposite of social realism. Realism with a string of pearls thrown in. Grimy life with fancy feathers. Poverty and pain with a horsehair wig. These blues sisters of Bessie Smith all knew how to dress, how to reach out to a full audience and let the blues rip.

The 'classic' blues singers followed in the royal footsteps of the Voodoo Queens and they signalled the emergence of a new type of record. They even gave themselves royal names: Clara Smith was 'Queen of the Moaners'; Bessie Smith was the 'Empress of the Blues'; Mamie Smith was the 'Queen of the Blues'; Ida Cox was the 'Uncrowned Queen of the Blues'; Ma Rainey was the 'Golden Necklace of the Blues' as well as being the 'Songbird of the South' and 'Mother of the Blues'. (Ma Rainey's famous necklace was made from gold coins of different sizes, from two-dollar-fifty pieces to heavy twenty-dollar eagles. She often kept her necklace in bed with her in case of theft.) These names were used in the billings for the concerts through the South, but they were also used by the people, the blues admirers and fans. Columbia may have promoted Bessie Smith as 'Queen of the Blues', but it was the people who called her 'Empress', the people who travelled all over to get to hear those women sing their blues. The people who crowded the streets and were moved on by the police in the heyday of the blueswomen, when hundreds were left waiting outside. Those people would have said, 'I went to see the Empress,' and everybody would have known who they were talking about. The classic blues singers were the first and only American black royal family. Ruby Walker said:

> Bessie was a queen. I mean, the people looked up to her and worshipped her like she was a queen. You know, she would walk into a room or out on a stage and people couldn't help but notice her – she was that kind of woman, a strong, beautiful woman with a personality as big as a house.[24]

All things are possible: the poor girl from Chattanooga can put on a silk gown and transform herself into an empress; she can wear a lampshade-fringe crown. There is the perception, on the one hand, of the blues as lowlife (the view of middle-class jazz fans and critics) and on the other

hand, the blues as high life, royalty (for classic blues singers and their fans). This combination can't be bettered: the
result is a black working-class queen. No ordinary queen
who has inherited somebody else's lineage quite by chance,
but a diva with style, daring, panache, imagination and
talent. A queen who knows how to shimmy. A queen who
can send herself up. A queen who can holler and shout. A
queen who knows what it is all about. A Queen of Tragedy;
a Queen of Bad Men; a Queen of Poverty; a Queen of the
Jail House. A queen who understands and has been through
herself everything that other ordinary people, particularly
ordinary *women*, have been through. A Queen of the Folk.
No wonder the classic Bessie Smith and the other Blues
Queens were so loved.

The touch of class, artistry and imagination that went
into the look and style of the classic blues singers is often
devalued or misunderstood, Alan Lomax writes:

With few exceptions, only women in show business,
women of questionable reputation, women who
flaunted their loose living, publicly performed the
blues – women like Mamie Smith, Bessie Smith and
Memphis Minnie. The list isn't very long. These
female blues singers toured the black vaudeville circuits
or performed in city nightclubs . . . They did not sing
in the street or play in jukes and barrooms, where they
would inevitably be subjected to sexual advances of
every sort . . .[25]

Many people perceived the blueswomen to be vulgar, crude, lewd, common, rough, raucous, lowlife. The subject matter of the songs, the double entendres, the kitchen man, the butcher man and the jelly roll didn't help the image either. There is lots of 'rough' in the songs of the classic blues singers. Songs like Alberta Hunter's 'I Want a Two-fisted, Double-jointed, Rough-and-ready Man'; Ida Cox's 'Wild Women Don't Have the Blues'; Ma Rainey's 'Rough and Tumble Blues'; Victoria Spivey's 'I Got Men All Over This Town'; Bessie Smith's 'Dirty No-Gooder Blues'. The classic blues singers took men as their central subject and wrote songs about what swines they were, how they cheated, lied, deceived and beat you up. Men in women's blues songs do not look good; they do not look good at all. The odd good man has got to be held on to at all costs because the blueswomen recognise what a rarity he is – 'Don't Fish in My Sea'. In sending men up, mocking and deriding them, the classic blues singers were revolutionary. They took control of their own image, and their songs relentlessly told the truth about no-good men. Male blues songs about women are actually quite mild by comparison. Michele Wallace in *Invisibility Blues* believes that classic blues singing is 'critical to defining the spectrum of possibilities for black women beyond servility and self-abnegation'.[26]

Although the classic blues singers performed on the vaudeville circuit and the TOBA circuit, often appearing at the same theatre halls or in the same tent shows to notices that proclaimed they were in town, it was years before their voices were actually recorded. The wax versions were a long time coming, considering Bessie Smith had been on the road and drawing a crowd since 1912 and Ma Rainey since 1902. In fact one of the earliest references to a woman singing a blues is to be found in *Songsters and Saints*:

Among the earliest recollections with a specific date was that of John Jacob Niles who, in 1898 heard Ophelia Simpson, known as 'Black Alfalfa'. She did the current ragtime things but was most effective in the native blues. Earlier she had killed her man, one Henry 'Dead Dog' Simpson, who worked at a fertilizer plant on the Ohio River near Louisville. After a brief period in the 'Stony Lonesome' jail, Ophelia worked for Dr Parker's Medicine Show where 'she cooked, helped mix the tape-worm eradicator and shouted in the oleo'. It was there that Niles heard her sing:

'I ain't got not a friend in dis town
Cause my New Orleans partner done turned me down
Po gal wishin' for dat jail-house key,
To open up de door and let herself go free.'[27]

'Nobody Knows You When You're Down and Out', 'Jail House Blues' and many other Bessie Smith classics perhaps owe their debt to Ophelia and Dead Dog Simpson. Or maybe not. The blues that the blueswomen sang – and

Bessie was only one of them – all conveyed this epic sense of life. They feature characters who are representative rather than extraordinary. The man in the blues songs could be anyman just like the woman singing about him could be anywoman. The blueswomen could sing, act, dance, hip-shake, shout, perform, draw a crowd, and at the same time be singing about ordinary life. Black women began to sing about their own personal problems, about the everyday; anything could crop up in a blues. The subject of Bessie Smith's first recording hit was a mistreating man. On wax, he is Bessie's first in a long, long line of mistreating men, mistreating Mama all the time.

There are many stories about how Bessie Smith came to make her first record. Frank Walker – who was in charge of the Columbia record company's 'race list' of records by black artists – tells it like this:

> I don't think there could have been more than fifty
> people up North who had heard about Bessie Smith
> when I sent Clarence Williams down South to get
> her . . . I told Clarence about the Smith girl and said,
> 'This is what you've got to do. go down there and find
> her and bring her back up here.'[28]

This is apparently untrue, since only two weeks earlier she was being rejected by the Okeh company in New York. Clarence Williams only had to go as far as South Philadelphia to bring her to Frank Walker. The idea of

Clarence Williams being sent all the way to the ramshackle cabin in Chattanooga and bringing a poor black girl with an already legendary voice straight into a recording studio belongs to the American Dream.

According to Frank Walker, the girl that Clarence brought back from the Deep South was no dream singer. 'She looked anything but a singer. She looked about seventeen – tall and fat and scared to death – just awful.'[29] In fact this was 1923 and Bessie was twenty-nine. She had already been on the road for eleven years and had built up huge audiences in the clubs in the South who threw extra money to tip her. Ethel Waters said Bessie's shouting brought worship wherever she worked. She was earning $50 to $75 a week – 'big money for our kind of vaudeville'. And Ma Rainey and her like would have influenced Bessie's style of dress. But maybe she did arrive in the studio looking like a teenager, tall and fat and scared to death.

Bessie Smith's records were made very early on when recordings were done acoustically. Her voice would travel through the large conical horn; at the other end the stylus would wait to be activated by the sound. The stylus made the appropriate impressions while cutting a groove in a thick wax-like disc. (The old phonographs, with their big horn, simply reversed the procedure to provide playback.) The thick wax discs would then be processed into metal masters from which test pressings were made. The record company would then choose which version of the song they thought to be the most successful. (Editing was not technically possible in those early days.) Bessie travelled throughout the South and the Midwest with a portable mock-up of this strange-looking acoustic recording equipment. She'd explain to her audiences how records were made by singing into the big horn as if she were actually recording. She chose many of her live songs from her recorded material in order to boost record sales.

It is incredible that Bessie's first recording was not made until 1923, since she auditioned for recording companies as early as 1921. The Black Swan company, which proudly presented its discs as 'The Only Genuine Colored Record – Others Are Only Passing for Colored', turned Bessie down. This was the company that was founded that same year by composer W. C. Handy, since dubbed the 'Father of the Blues' – but he was never married to Ma Rainey! It was the first black-owned record company and was sold to the public as such. However, Bessie Smith's voice was the wrong colour even for them. They wouldn't take the risk. They thought her voice too 'rough'. (For rough, read 'black'.) The very qualities that make her voice still live on today – rough, raw, harsh – were loathed by Black Swan. They preferred the smooth tones of an Ethel Waters. From news reports at the time, it appears that the Emerson Company and the Okeh label also judged her style too 'rough'. Bessie Smith's voice and skin were not the only aspects of her that the recording companies considered too dark or rough. There was her behaviour. One story has it that she failed a test with Black Swan Records because she interrupted a song with, 'Hold on, let me spit!' and the president of the company immediately ended the audition.[30]

Bessie, even then, was no stranger to being turned down for being too rough or too dark. Irving C. Miller, who threw her out of his chorus line in 1912 for being too black-skinned, told Humphrey Lyttelton, 'She was a natural singer even then – but we stressed beauty in the chorus line and Bessie did not meet my standards as far as looks were concerned.' The advertising slogan of Miller's shows speaks volumes: 'Glorifying the Brownskin Girls'. (It was this same impresario who had no hesitation in booking Bessie's rival, Gertrude Saunders, years later.) Light-skinned black women were favoured for a very long time.

I remember being in a school show when I was eight. We were doing the dances Bessie could do so brilliantly, such as the Black Bottom and the Charleston. I remember not being able to get my steps right and my teacher saying, 'I thought you'd be good at this. I thought you people had it in your blood.' The comment made me lie awake at night, wondering what was in my blood. I don't know what the girls from Balmuildy Primary were doing learning such lewd dances in any case. I find it difficult to connect the history of the Charleston with my Scottish primary school. (An early example of multiculturalism.) As Humphrey Lyttelton explains:

In the early years of the century the population of the San Juan Hill area [of Harlem] was boosted by an influx of migrants from the South, some from Alabama, some from the part of South Carolina and Georgia that centered around Charleston. From the testimony of both The Lion and James P., it is clear that these latter people, known as Gullahs or Geechies, had a powerful effect on the style of the local piano men . . . 'They danced cakewalks and cotillions; by this time we had learned to play the natural twelve-bar blues that evolved from the spirituals . . . the Gullahs would start out early in the evening dancing two-steps, waltzes, schottisches; but as the night wore on and the liquor began to work, they would start improvising their own steps and that was when they wanted us to get-in-the-alley, real lowdown . . . it was from the improvised steps that the Charleston dance originated.'[31]

Bessie Smith was born, lived and died in a country obsessed with colour. A country that could never shake off the legacy of slavery, of segregation. The systems of slavery and racism in the United States ensured that a person with even a 'drop' of 'black blood' was considered black. Racism could not tolerate any deviation from 'pure whiteness'. Racism required white people and black people to keep absolutely separate. Any 'mixing' of the two races was regarded with suspicion. This obsession with colour and blood, and the colour of blood, manifests itself in countless ways, not least in the culture of the people. You get a sense of a country's laws by listening to the music, reading the literature and looking at the art. As late as the Second World War, the American Red Cross, though well aware that all human blood is the same, kept blood plasma segregated by race. As explained by Geneviève Fabre and Robert O'Meally in *History and Memory in African-American Culture*, here is a country that, not content with separating the living, had to separate the dead:

> There were even segregated railway compartments for the deceased. In 1835 a railroad was planned for the transport of corpses and mourners from St Claude Street to the Cemetery at the Bayou St John in New Orleans. The city council stipulated that the contractor had to provide separate cars for white, free colored and slave corpses, with fees ranging from fifty cents for slaves to three dollars for whites.[32]

The recording companies in the early 1920s could not have anticipated a blues boom. Black Swan, the company that promoted black artists, wanted its singers to possess a light tone, a light touch, a light shade. The blues were dark, rough, brutal and real, and all the major companies underestimated their marketability. But suddenly the blues were big business.

On record, Bessie's blues made an incredible and immediate impact. People who had migrated from the South to the North rushed out to buy her records, because her phrasing and words reminded them of home. Downhome talk. She filled people with awe and longing. With a sense of themselves. Black people identified with her songs. She was like a preacher in the way she affected people. Guitarist Danny Barker explains:

> Bessie Smith was a fabulous deal to watch. She was a pretty large woman and she could sing the blues. She had a church deal mixed up in it. She dominated a stage. You didn't turn your head when she went on, you just watched Bessie . . . She just upset you. When you say Bessie – that was it. She was unconscious of her surroundings. She never paid anybody any mind . . . She could bring about mass hypnotism. When she was performing, you could hear a pin drop.[33]

Bessie Smith lived an epic life. Her life could be painted on a broad canvas. She was big in stature, size and influence. She was *the people*. This ability to write songs, to record songs and perform songs that touched the heart of everyone who listened to her is what has kept her alive for so many years. She was her time. She totally reflects her time. She had some pair of lungs and could fill a massive hall with her voice. She didn't need a microphone. She just belted those blues out. As Buster Bailey said, 'There was none of this whispering jive.' (A hilarious description of someone like Betty Carter.) The fascinating thing about the voice of Bessie Smith, for all its blueness, is its total lack of sentimentality. She can sing unnerving, sad songs without

a note of self-pity. It is the very flatness of her voice, singing about tragedies, that so moves us. It is not in any way
the voice of a victim. It is unrefined. It is not sweet, sugary.
It is not smooth. So why did the record companies initially
reject her? Her voice was that of an ordinary working-class
black woman. And they didn't think that the voice of an
ordinary working-class black woman could or would ever
sell records. They were, of course, wrong because they
underestimated the amount of ordinary working-class
black women that would buy Bessie Smith and the other
blueswomen's records. They didn't realise that ordinary
black people would so identify with the blues that the blues
would seem to be the singing version of their lives. It was
this that made the records of Mamie Smith, Bessie Smith,
Ma Rainey, Alberta Hunter, Ida Cox, Victoria Spivey
and others so popular and, with Bessie Smith at least, so
long-lasting.

It took two days for Bessie to conquer her nerves when
she first turned up on 15 February 1923 at the Columbia
studio to record 'Downhearted Blues' and 'Gulf Coast
Blues'. Arriving, 'tall, fat and scared to death', the Queen
of the Blues did not make the wax the first day of recordings. She tried 'T'ain't Nobody's Business' nine times
and failed, and she tried 'Downhearted Blues' twice
and failed. Maybe it was her nerves or maybe it was that
strange conical horn which stuck out from a drapery-cov-
ered wall. The effect must have been quite sinister. Bessie
probably didn't trust the damn thing. Maybe she thought

she'd lose herself in that big hole. Maybe she thought they ought to be able to record her differently. Maybe her head was full of bad memories of all the previous times she had been in recording studios and been rejected. She might have been at a total loss without her live audience throwing money, shouting and stomping for more. She might have found the studio cold. She might have been stone-cold sober. Imagine her in that studio in 1923, wearing the red dress that Jack pawned his pocket watch to buy, making her first ever record. Could she have realised the significance of her break into wax? Did she fear she'd lose her talent through having her live voice recorded and transmuted to wax? A waxwork? A dummy? She possibly mistrusted the whole technological thing, such as it was then. She might have felt she was being had. But she soon got the hang of it. Humphrey Lyttelton says: 'The singing that was transmitted to wax was, from the outset, mature, steeped in harsh experience and formidably commanding.'[34]

The sales of 'Downhearted Blues' – three quarters of a million copies in six months – far exceeded the sales of any other blues record. The black public were eager to purchase records through mail-order catalogues, record stores in black neighbourhoods or even through the Pullman porters. The blues sold both in the North and in the South and became part of the record companies' 'race records' series, as Paul Oliver explains:

The term 'Race records' for issues directed solely to the black purchaser was in use by Okeh as early as January 1922. Several other major record companies began to issue Race series: Columbia commenced in 1921 while Paramount . . . merged with the only label to have black ownership, Black Swan, and commenced its Race series in 1922 . . . By the end of 1922 Race records were being distributed in many Northern cities and as far south as Alabama.[35]

In the South the blues sold to black and white people; in the more 'liberal' North, they just sold to black people. It is possible to have been white in the North in the 1920s and never have known that blues records even existed. This is because in the North, advertising of so-called 'Race records' was restricted to the black press, and the distribution of the records took place only in black areas. Southerners, though, became part of the 'race market'. White and black people, though segregated, crowded into those tents to hear the blues. Bessie Smith gave many performances in 'whites only' theatres where she changed neither the style of her music nor its contents. She refused to 'water herself down'. It is interesting to me, though, that she should have played in those theatres at all. I would have thought she would have refused as a matter of principle. But maybe that is naive; maybe she had no choice.

Bessie was at the height of her popularity after her first records were released. Everywhere she went it was the same story. People had heard Bessie's records and now they wanted to hear her in person. Five records were now on the market: 'Downhearted Blues', 'Gulf Coast Blues', 'Aggravatin' Papa', 'Beale Street Mama' and 'Baby, Won't You Please Come Home'. Her reputation had grown beyond all expectations. Columbia were dazzled by her success. Bessie was now making $350 a week from personal appearances. During her tour in June 1923, streets in Atlanta were blocked and hundreds of fans were unable to gain entrance to the theatre. The crowds, wild and hysterical, pushing and crushing, fought to get to her next performance as ten policemen tried to keep things under control. At this early stage in her recording career Bessie Smith already had the kind of star status that we associate with today's pop icons.

Once Bessie had recorded her version of a song, it practically wiped out all others. Ida Cox wrote 'Graveyard Dream Blues' and recorded it with Lovie Austin's Blues Serenaders in June 1923. Three months later, Bessie Smith recorded the same song for a January release, but Columbia decided to rush it out for competitive reasons. Paramount then fought back with Ida Cox releasing yet another version of 'Graveyard Dream Blues' after Bessie's. In this way, the record companies pitted one blues singer against another in the search for total domination of the market. Bessie Smith sang a lot of songs that had previously been sung by other blueswomen because in those days there was no copyright over songs. 'Chicago Bound Blues' was another Ida Cox number that Bessie then recorded. 'Downhearted Blues', her first release, was originally an Alberta Hunter number.

In 1923 Bessie recorded song after song after song. Columbia signed her up for a lucrative eight-year contract. Between 1923 and 1931, she recorded 160 songs with Columbia, roughly twenty a year. Bessie Smith wrote and composed thirty-seven of these blues. She was right there at the beginning of the recording industry, in and out of studios like there was no tomorrow. Any time she came back from a tour, she was whisked into a studio to record another number. During that period, she worked alongside some of the best musicians of her day: Fletcher Henderson, Louis Armstrong, Fred Longshaw, Jack Teagarden, James P. Johnson, Coleman Hawkins, Joe Smith. But the most exciting combination musically was Bessie Smith and Louis Armstrong, in those sessions they recorded on 14 January 1925. 'Reckless Blues', 'Cold in Hand Blues', 'Sobbin' Hearted Blues' and 'You've Been A Good Ole Wagon' were all recorded that day. It has turned out to be one of the most memorable dates in the history of the blues. Louis Armstrong's horn understood Bessie perfectly. They are totally at ease with each other. There is all the awesome complexity of perfect harmony between the two of them. Her big blues voice and his big horn.

Neither Bessie Smith nor any of the other classic blues singers received royalties for their songs back then. They were paid per usable side; the amount varied depending on their popularity. At her peak, Bessie could earn as much as $200 per usable side. She was the best paid of all the classic blueswomen. She was on a rollercoaster and that rollercoaster was her blues. Five of her records were on the market, and her reputation had grown beyond all expectations. But success would not last. After the Wall Street Crash of 1929 and the Depression, a new combo style of blues became fashionable. 'Urban blues' or 'Chicago blues' then dominated the scene from the mid-1930s through the 1940s. The likes of Muddy Waters and Howlin' Wolf took off; the classic blues singers were replaced by men with acoustic guitars.

I dream of a place between your breasts
to build my house like a haven
where I plant crops
in your body
an endless harvest
where the commonest rock
is moonstone and ebony opal
giving milk to all of my hungers
and your night comes down upon me
like a nurturing rain.

Audre Lorde, 'Woman'

# RUBY ON THE ROAD

My best friend, Gillian Innes, loved Bessie Smith. We spent many hours in Gillian's bedroom, imitating Bessie Smith and Pearl Bailey. Various objects served as microphones from hairbrushes to wooden spoons. At the age of twelve, singing Pearl Bailey's 'Tired of the life I lead, / Tired of the blues I breed, / I'm tired, mighty tired of you,' or Bessie Smith's 'You've got to give me some, please give me some,' was a way of expressing our wild emotions for each other. The one who was singing looked directly at the other, getting completely into the mood of the blues, making her body movements correspond to the words. The one who was watching killed herself laughing. Gillian's box bedroom floor was our centre stage. She had her own old gramophone in the corner. We'd rush to it as soon as the number was over to play it again and swap the singer. The singer would then jump onto the bed and become the whole audience. We fancied each other singing those blues. She could make one eyebrow raise itself way above the other. I was besotted with her and the blues. First love; I was positive Gillian would grow up to be a famous singer. My life at that age was charged with all the intense devotion and loyalty of a schoolgirl crush. I could barely breathe. The air in her box bedroom was thick with secrets. The door firmly shut. Our own private performance. Gillian lent me a book about Bessie when we were thirteen or so. I never found that book again, but I remember reading about Bessie travelling in her Pullman, which I then imagined as a sort of wagon, like one of those wagons on the Oregon trail. I imagined it to have little windows with red curtains bunched to the side. I read in this book that Bessie had sex with women on the road. I could barely contain myself. Who did she have sex with? What were the women's names? She got to sing the blues. She had a beautiful haunting voice. She got to travel in the Deep South. And she got to have sex with chorus girls on the road in her own Pullman. What more could a girl want? It must have been a bumpy ride. I remember the name Ruby. The name Ruby coming up all the time.

Ruby Walker was Jack Gee's niece. Her relationship with her aunt, Bessie Smith, was undoubtedly one of the most crucial in Bessie's life. It was possibly even more significant and complex than Bessie's relationship with Jack himself. As far as we know, Bessie Smith never had sex with Ruby, though their relationship has all the complexity of a sexual one. They were companions from before Bessie made her first record in 1923 until Jack and Bessie's marriage broke up in 1929. Bessie spent far more time with Ruby than she did with her husband. It is certainly true to say that Ruby Walker knew and understood Bessie better than anybody. She was all things to Bessie: her travelling companion, her confidante, her keeper. At various points in their nomadic showbiz life, Ruby acted as decoy, as a red herring; she would lie for her, spy for her, risk her own neck for her. Her most fascinating role in the life of Bessie Smith was as the keeper of her lesbian secrets. Bessie kept nothing from Ruby. She knew every intimate detail of Bessie's travelling promiscuity. But she kept schtum. On numerous occasions, she ran away with Bessie to avoid the wrath of Jack.

The first time Ruby heard Bessie Smith sing it changed her life. 'I didn't know it then,' she said, 'but that's what happened.' It was in New York, February 1923. Bessie and Jack were staying in Jack's mother's house on 132nd Street between Fifth and Lenox Avenues. Above 132nd Street was a Harlem full of black people, and the home of the writers, artists and musicians of the Harlem Renaissance. Harlem had a dazzling night-life which would have suited Bessie Smith down to the ground. The young Duke Ellington described Harlem as having 'the world's most glamorous atmosphere'. Bessie spent the days at 132nd Street rehearsing for her first recording. Ruby Walker first heard Bessie Smith sing in Jack's mother's living room.

Ruby was bowled over by Bessie's voice. After that initial meeting, she persuaded Bessie to let her come with her on her tours. Not only did she want the glamour and excitement of Bessie Smith's life, she wanted to *be* Bessie Smith. So Bessie took Ruby on the road, teaching her simple dancing steps until Ruby became part of her show, performing in the intervals when Bessie was making one of her elaborate costume changes. Ruby had very high hopes for herself as a singer, but unfortunately she never managed to become a star in her own right. She recognised Bessie's genius and for the most part contented herself by hanging out with it, in the hope that some of it might rub off on her.

Ruby travelled with Bessie from Cincinnati to Chattanooga, from Pittsburgh to Philadelphia, from New York to New Orleans, from Birmingham to Baltimore, from Detroit to Dallas. Ruby didn't just get to see a lot of America with her blues guide, she also discovered that Bessie knew just about every nightspot and every small bar in the country. Initially, they travelled from city to city by car, bus or train until, in 1925, Bessie's brother came up with the idea of buying her own personal railroad car. It was custom-made by the Southern Iron and Equipment Company in Atlanta and painted bright yellow with green lettering. Her fans could tell when Bessie had arrived the minute they saw the yellow train pull into their station. Bessie's Pullman became as notorious as she was. When the Empress arrived in town, she did it with the style and glamour that people associated with her. The train was as vital to her image as the rhinestones or the plumes. Ruby loved the train. It was seventy-eight feet long. It had seven staterooms – each one could sleep four – and a lower level that could accommodate up to thirty-five people. It had a kitchen and a bathroom with hot and cold running water. The long corridor carried the show tent's central pole. A room at the back of the train carried the canvas, along with the case-loads of peanuts, crackerjacks and soft drinks that Bessie sold on the road. The whole crew lived on the train.

They didn't have to split up when they hit a town; the train was big enough for all of them. Maud Smith said to Chris Albertson:

> I'll never forget it. It was Clarence's idea to buy the car, and it was delivered to us in a small town near Atlanta on a sunny Monday. Everybody was so excited, and we laughed and carried on as we walked through the car and examined every corner. And what a difference it made – some of the towns we hit didn't have hotels for us so we used to have to spread out, one staying here, another one there. Now we could just live on the train.[36]

Travelling life on the train was easier than before. For one thing, they didn't have to confront racism on the road so often, or stay at bed-and-breakfast dives, way out of town. In the 1920s, no black person, not even a superstar, could stay at even a third-rate hotel, never mind a decent one. The only hotels that would take in black people were bed-and-breakfast places and rooming houses. It was possible to be as famous as Bessie Smith and still be the victim of racism. America might be proud of its blues tradition now, but it certainly did not help blues performers when they needed it. Touring the racist South was a nightmare for the blues performer. The Ku Klux Klan were at their height in the 1920s, exactly the same time as the heyday of the classic blueswomen. (Interestingly, the Klan's decline began in the

1930s too.) But in the Pullman, there was privacy, autonomy and plenty of space. You could have your own food, often cooked by the Empress herself. Bessie Smith made stews for her entire troupe, pigs' feet or other Southern specialities. She prepared the food in the galley of the railroad car. Sometimes the musicians would be drafted in to peel potatoes. Sometimes, when the weather was fine, they would have a picnic somewhere near the track where the railroad car was stationed.

The sleeping quarters were tight. Everyone knew everyone else's business. Ruby knew all of Bessie's business. Bessie frequently had sexual relationships with women on the road. There was Marie, Lillian and countless others; none were hidden from the other musicians, prop boys and crew. But nobody spilled the beans. Everybody protected her when Jack came. She threatened to throw them out of her show if anyone so much as breathed a word to Jack. Everyone was so terrified of muscular Jack, with the powerful and unrepentant fists, that no one would have said anything anyway.

On the road, away from Jack, Bessie had the freedom to be herself. She could drink good moonshine as much as she liked. She could go to buffet party after buffet party and watch all manner of lewd sex acts. She could be promiscuous, having sex with young men and young women on the road. She could go out after her shows and not return 'till the break of day'. She tried to keep it all secret from her ex-nightwatchman husband, but he often caught her red-handed by turning up unexpectedly and surprising her. On one particular occasion, on closing night after the show, everyone changed into their nightgowns and pyjamas, as was their custom, parading from room to room in a hotel they were staying in, eating Bessie's food and drinking homemade gin. They wound up in Bessie's room on the first floor. Marie, a young ballet dancer, was wearing bright red pyjamas, a gift from Bessie. (Bessie often bought the women in her life red gifts. She bought Ruby a pair of red dancing shoes.) Marie was dancing around in her pyjamas to Bessie's shouts. Ruby passed out. She was always the first to pass out at such parties. The next thing she knew Marie was tearing down the corridor, followed by Bessie at her heels. Jack had caught Bessie in bed with Marie. The two of them huddled together in a corner of Ruby's room, hiding from Jack. He passed by the door, shouting, 'Come out of there, I'm going to kill you tonight, you bitch.' Jack went off into the street looking for Bessie. Bessie waited a while and then gathered her whole troupe together and rushed for her Pullman. Many of them left their belongings in the hotel, they were in such a hurry to escape Jack. They all got on the train. The Empress was still in her pyjamas as the train pulled out of Detroit, heading towards Columbus, Ohio. 'That's how I lost the only fur coat I ever had,' Ruby told Chris Albertson.[37] (Needless to say, the fur coat was a gift from Bessie.)

But Jack caught up with them, as he always did. His life, policing his wife, must have been pretty exciting too. He would stalk them, tracking them down until he managed to have a piece of Bessie. It probably wasn't jealousy any longer that fuelled him, but a desire for power and control. His wife's life was completely out of hand. There wasn't much he could do about it. He caught up with Bessie in Columbus and came into her dressing room before the show to tell her that he was going to beat her up afterwards. Bessie rushed everybody through the grand finale, changed into ordinary clothes and dashed for the station with Ruby, where the two of them caught the next train for Cincinnati. The rest of the musicians were dumped on the road. (Bessie frequently abandoned her musicians, leaving them penniless in Detroit or Dallas. She had a reputation for treating her musicians badly, in contrast to her generosity towards friends and family.)

When Bessie took off like this, to escape the wrath of Jack, she always took Ruby too. Not her current woman lover, but Ruby. Only Ruby; everyone else could go to hell. No wonder the other chorus girls were jealous of her. (Once a chorus girl shredded a pair of new dancing shoes that Bessie had just bought Ruby.) Why did she not dump Ruby too? Ruby was Bessie's right-hand woman. She was the one who planned, who covered for her, who lied to Jack for her. She was the one who would get on the phone to Jack the morning after a night before to tell him that Bessie was unwell. Sometimes, Bessie would actually throw herself down the stairs so that she could have genuine injuries in an attempt to avoid being beaten up by Jack.

Ruby's undying admiration for Bessie is not puzzling. But was Ruby admired by Bessie? Did she desire Ruby all those years? Did she see Ruby as unobtainable because she was Jack's niece and Jack would have gone wild at the combination of the two of them? Did Jack originally tell Ruby to tour with Bessie so that she could spy on her for him? Perhaps Ruby was feeding Jack information about his wife, until she fell for Bessie herself. The fact that their relationship was never consummated, while Bessie had frequent relationships with other women, is interesting. Many of the women Bessie travelled with had lesbian relationships. Nobody was hung up about it. Yet Bessie did not want Ruby to have sex with anybody. If Bessie couldn't have her, nobody else could. She told Ruby she would throw her off her show if she caught her having sex with anybody.

Perhaps Bessie liked Ruby's devotion without sex. Perhaps she needed her in a different way; a constant presence to give her life security, stability, a sense of belonging. Perhaps she knew that Ruby loved her more than anyone else did. More than her own sisters. Perhaps Ruby reminded her of her sisters when they were young. Bessie enjoyed fooling around with Ruby, joking and laughing. She enjoyed shopping for Ruby, stunning her with one lavish gift after another. It's quite possible that without Ruby, Bessie wouldn't have managed to get her show on the road at all.

Ruby was Bessie's accomplice. She aided and abetted Bessie's lesbianism, covering for her and inventing stories for her. Was she in love with Bessie herself? Everything she says about Bessie is drenched in admiration. 'No one messed with Bessie Smith . . . She was a strong woman with a beautiful strong constitution and she loved a good time.'[38] She even compares Bessie to a real queen.

Ruby Walker idolised Bessie Smith. She loved the way she looked; the way she sang; the way she drank; the way she partied; the way she cussed; the way she fought; the way she danced; the way she spent money. Ruby loved everything about Bessie . . . She loved her so much she wanted to be her. But Bessie could be violent if she strayed. Once Ruby tried sleeping with a young man that Bessie was also sleeping with. When Bessie found out she beat Ruby up. The boy in question was called Agie Pitts, a handsome young dancer from Detroit. Bessie caught Ruby in the dressing room with Agie Pitts and flew into a rage. She told Ruby that she was going to break her out of the habit of trying to be Bessie Smith. She told her she was going to let her know that she ain't Bessie Smith. She beat Ruby up so badly that Ruby's screams attracted the police and all three of them, Ruby, Agie and Bessie, ended up in jail. The dressing-room scene is like an early black version of *All About Eve*.

*I caught that girl red-handed trying to be me. She was sitting in my dressing room looking at herself queerly in the mirror. It made my blood boil. She was trying to look sad. She was so in herself that she didn't even notice me. And she did this weird thing with her eyebrows, bringing them in on each other, like they was commiserating with each other over somebody's death. I don't think I ever look that bad. But there she was in the mirror trying to be me. Then she closed her eyes and sang 'Mama's crossed the danger line'. She must have sensed me right behind her. The real fucking thing. 'Cause when she opened her eyes, Ruby did startle. I say going up behind her all quiet like and pulling her long hair to the side, 'What on earth you up to, girl? Eh?' She say nothing. She chuckles some. Which is aggravating. I grab hold of that lump of black hair some more. She thinks she's cute 'cause her hair is practically straight as her nose. I get a hold of it and I just pull lumps of the stuff out. I will destroy you, bitch, before I let you be me, I say and walk out. But when I'm in the corridor, I hear her start up again, softly, this time singing, 'St Louis gal, look what you done done,' and I go back in and she's wearing my dress and she's dancing, swaying side to side like I do. I go up to her and I hold her hips and she takes me into her dance and I kiss her. It's the first time I have ever kissed her. I don't think I have ever had a kiss like it in my life. We lost all time in that kiss. We was dreaming, slow and soft. Her lips full and wet, moving with me, tracing my lips, finding my tongue. It was all so slow, so slow. We could have become something else in that kiss. I forgot the room, and where I was. I closed my eyes. I don't usually close my eyes, but the one time I ever kissed Ruby Walker, I closed my eyes. It was like kissing myself.*

Many of the women performers that Bessie travelled with were lesbians. Some were even married lesbians. Boula Lee, a chorus girl, was the wife of the Harlem Frolics music director, Bill Woods. Boula Lee fancied Ruby Walker and once thought she saw another woman making a pass at her. She attacked Ruby, telling her that she shouldn't mess around with 'them other bitches'. Then she leaned forward and scratched Ruby's face. Right on cue, Jack turned up, demanding an explanation for his niece's scratched face. Bill Woods, totally unaware of his wife's preference for women, retorted, 'It was one of them bulldaggers who is after Ruby.' The irony was too much for Bessie Smith to take. She said, 'What do you mean, one of them? It was your wife.' When Jack caught up with Boula, he threw her down the stairs.

At that time, Bessie was having a serious relationship with Lillian, another of the women in her show. It was January 1927 and the troupe were in St Louis at the Booker Washington Theatre. Ruby and Lillian were sharing a room. Bessie entered the room and kissed Lillian in front of Ruby, from whom she had nothing to hide. Lillian, embarrassed, tried to pull herself away, admonishing Bessie for her public display. Bessie told her that she had twelve women on the show and could have 'one every night' if she wanted to; she then ignored Lillian for several days. Lillian took the cold shoulder for three nights. But on the fourth night, she did not turn up at the theatre. Maud Smith noticed a letter sticking out from under Lillian's door. It was a suicide note.

Without taking time to read the note, Bessie, with Ruby
and Maud at her heels, ran next door to the hotel. When
they reached Lillian's door, they smelled gas. Bessie tried
to force the door, panicked, rushed downstairs and got
the proprietor. When he let them in, they found Lillian
lying across the bed, unconscious. The proprietor had to
break the windowpanes: Lillian had nailed the window
shut. She was taken to the nearest hospital . . . 'From
that day on,' says Ruby, 'she didn't care where or when
Bessie kissed her – she got real bold.'[39]

When Bessie went on tour in the South or the Midwest,
it wasn't so much a tour of the blues as a tour of the bars.
Bessie knew every backstreet and every bar there was to
know in any given town. There wasn't a bar anywhere that
hadn't made the Empress's acquaintance. Ruby was constantly impressed with her repertoire. Bessie also knew
every buffet flat. Buffet flats, also known as goodtime flats,
were small, private establishments offering illicit pastimes
from gambling to sex shows, to a variety of sex acts. They
were a variation on whorehouses, with a more upmarket
clientele. They provided 'important persons' with their
sexual equals, judging for themselves who would go with
whom. You could always get good bootleg at a buffet flat.
Bessie went to one in Detroit while she was performing at
the Koppin Theatre. She took five of her girls along with
her. Before she went, she said her mantra: 'Don't tell Jack.'
Ruby describes the scene:

It was nothing but faggots and bulldykers, a real open house. Everything went on in that house – tongue baths, you name it. They called them buffet flats because buffet means everything, everything that was in the life. Bessie was well known in that place.[40]

Ruby's tone here is slightly lofty, as if she herself were above it all. Yet she went along. Everywhere Bessie Smith went, Ruby Walker went too. She admired Bessie's penchant for the night-life, Bessie's supreme talent for finding a good drink. The Empress was famous for liking the rough bootleg stuff. She was still drinking the bad stuff even when the good stuff became legal again. Like just about everything else in life, Bessie liked it rough. In Atlanta, the garbageman sold alcohol in the streets. He went up and down neighbourhoods with a huge can on wheels, shouting 'Garbageman. Garbageman.' People would run out with their glasses in hand and get them filled. Bessie didn't buy from the garbageman, however, because she drank a great deal more than just a glass. She went to a man who lived under the viaduct who sold bad liquor by the half gallon.

I'm a young woman and ain't done runnin' round,
I'm a young woman and ain't done runnin' round.
Some people call me a hobo, some call me a bum,
Nobody knows my name, nobody knows what I've
    done.
I'm as good as any woman in your town,

118

I ain't no high yeller, I'm a beginner brown.
I ain't gonna marry, ain't gonna settle down,
I'm gonna drink good moonshine and run these browns
   down.

'Young Woman's Blues'

Ruby enjoyed the wild life with Bessie on the road. Hiding from Jack. Hanging out in bars and buffet flats. Learning the odd dance step in small moments between one hangover and the next. She liked the way that Bessie sang. The way every blues seemed to relate directly to her life. There was a line for everything: 'There'll be a hot time in the old town tonight'. Bessie chronicled her own life. Ruby, knowing the Empress better than anybody, recognised the landmarks. The woman who ran the buffet flat in Detroit is large as life in 'Soft Pedal Blues':

There's a lady in our neighbourhood who runs a buffet flat
And when she holds a party she knows just where she's at.
Have all the fun, ladies and gentlemen,
But please don't make it too long.

There's a wonderful 'Yahoo!' in the middle of this song, screamed out after she declares how drunk she is: 'I've got them soft pedalling blues.'

On the road, more of Bessie's talents went into her secret lesbian life (secret from Jack Gee only) than into her shows. Maybe it wouldn't have been quite so exciting if the danger of Jack discovering her had not been so present. Bessie carried out her lesbian relationships so openly that we all know about them still. She didn't mind anyone else knowing so long as they didn't tell Jack. She kissed Lillian in front of people. She didn't care what anybody said about her, ever. But she barely mentioned her own lesbianism in her songs. (Other blues singers, Ma Rainey amongst them, sang openly about lesbianism. But Bessie mostly sang about men.) Homosexuality is seen as something puzzling and strange in 'Foolish Man's Blues', and apart from that song there is hardly a reference to her own bisexuality in any of her other blues:

> There's two things got me puzzled, there's
> Two things I don't understand.
> There's two things got me puzzled, there's
> Two things I don't understand;
> That's a mannish-acting woman, and a
> Skipping, twistin', woman-acting man.
>
> 'Foolish Man Blues'

Did she marry a man because she feared her own lesbianism? Did she marry Jack because she wanted somebody to keep her in order, to make rules and stop her from drinking? Was she simply self-destructive, lavishing her love and her money on a man who could never return either, who ultimately ended up stealing both? It is interesting to consider what Bessie Smith's life would have been like if she had not been married to Jack, whether or not she would have had a more constant relationship with Lillian or Marie. Perhaps she thought that men were for marrying and women were for having on the road. Otherwise, why was she married in the first place? She was frequently unfaithful to Jack with both sexes. Chorus girls. Younger men. When she went home to Jack after an exhaustive tour – booze, sex and brawls – she'd try and cut out the drink, play the role of demure wife, quiet and calm, padding about in her slippers, talking to neighbours over the fence, cooking Jack big stews for his dinners. But it never lasted long. Wild Bessie always wanted out: 'I'm a young woman and ain't done runnin' round.' She was a wild woman and no Jack Gee was ever going to successfully tame her. Even after Jack left her, she didn't stop having relationships with men. She would have been free by then to concentrate solely on a relationship with a woman, but she didn't. Until the end of her life, she continued to have involvements with both sexes, to 'swing' both ways. It wasn't just jazz that could swing.

Ruby Walker's intimate relationship with Bessie Smith lasted the same length of time as Bessie's marriage to Jack. But when Jack left Bessie in 1929 for Gertrude Saunders, Ruby left too. She claimed that Jack forced her to join him and it is certainly true that she, like everyone else, feared him. Even so, Ruby's departure was a big betrayal. Bessie did not recover from the double blow. Ruby was present when Jack beat Bessie up in Columbus and she witnessed

Bessie's huge distress, but that did not stop her leaving too. After Jack left, he returned for a brief while to help Bessie work on her show at the Wallace Theatre in Indianapolis. Bessie was drunk all the time, totally devastated. She went off, leaving the whole troupe and not even taking Ruby with her this last time. So Jack tried to save the engagement by substituting Ruby for Bessie. They even padded her up to look fatter. Bessie heard about Ruby playing the part of the Empress and came back and ran Ruby off the stage. Perhaps Bessie stopped trusting Ruby right there and then. Ruby had always been ambitious for herself. Life with Bessie Smith did not give her many opportunities to be famous, as she had hoped. Bessie was content with Ruby doing dance routines, but she never wanted Ruby to sing. Ruby and Jack left to join Gertrude Saunders' show again, leaving Bessie to sing to herself: *Ain't nobody's blues but mine.*

I like to imagine that Bessie's great love of her life was Ruby Walker. I like to think that Ruby on the road was in love with Bessie all along. When she betrayed Bessie to join the Gertrude Saunders show, she never forgave herself. Her life had no meaning without the Empress riding her through the backstreets of Harlem in the dead of night. There was nothing to live for without Bessie's blues.

*Bessie,*

*I know you are reading this saying 'I ain't never heard of such shit!' But I'm going to do as I want to anyway, as you would say, and write this letter. I am sorry I am here*

with Jack. He made me come. You know we was always
frightened of him. He threatened me if I stayed in your
show. Anyhows I have just made one big mistake. The
biggest mistake of my life. This is Ruby talking. You know
I don't bullshit. I know you better than anybody. You are
still reading and laughing some despite yourself. I can
picture you holding on to this letter with one finger, holding
it some distance from yourself, your face grinning that wide
grin of yours when you whole mouth opens up. I like to kiss
you when your mouth opens up like that. I like to see the
way you eyes glint when I dance. You were surprised how
good I was at dancing. I don't know why I left you. I guess
I thought you never loved me as much as I loved you. I
remember the first time I heard you sing. I just stood there
and watched you and my whole life changed. I didn't know
it then, but that's what happened. My whole life changed
because of you, Bessie. I won't never love anyone like I
loved you and I want you to know it. So if you have kept
reading this letter of mine, you know it now. I don't expect
a reply. Though I'd like one. I'd like one more than I can
say. But I'll leave that down to you. I am yours, even
though I'm with Jack, I'm yours. The man has a power
over people. You know that better than anybody, don't you.
Why don't you come and get me and take me home. Why
don't you come. I wait and I watch out of this window here
but you ain't never appeared outside. I have tried to make
you, using the power of my mind. I imagine you coming for
me in a smart car, dressed up in your blue and white satin

*dress with the hoop skirt, your favourite. I see you with a deep red shawl round your shoulders and pearls round your neck. You've got a gift for me. You always was crazy about buying folks gifts. I open it up and inside the little jewellery box is a ring with a ruby stone. Come and get me. Don't you dare ever forget me.*

*Ruby xxx*

It is dangerous for a woman to defy the gods;
To taunt them with the tongue's thin tip,
Or strut in the weakness of mere humanity,
Or draw a line daring them to cross;
The gods own the searing lightning,
The drowning waters, tormenting fears
And anger of red sins.

Anne Spencer, 'Letter to My Sister'

# TALES OF THE EMPRESS

But the stories of her portentous rages, tempestuous love-affairs, wild bouts of generosity, epic binges and not infrequent recourse to devastating fisticuffs – all of which stretch back as far as her public career itself – leave us with the impression of a totally untamed creature who remained, to the end of her days, immune from the restraints of manners or convention.

Humphrey Lyttelton, *The Best of Jazz*

Bessie Smith's life lent itself to legends. Her life so aptly corresponded with her times that each seems emblematic of the other. She was successful and high in the roaring, manic 1920s; she was depressed and low in the down-to-earth-with-a-crash 1930s. At various points in her life, she exhibited perfect timing. She was there when blues made their shift from the backrooms and onto the stage; she was there at the beginning of the record industry; she was there at the beginning of the 'race records' promotions; she was there at the beginning of the jazz era. She was in Harlem during the Harlem Renaissance. She was with Louis Armstrong when he was just a wee boy, practically. She became poorer when the blues started to die. She sang 'Nobody Knows You When You're Down and Out' at a time that ensured it would be a classic forever, right after the Wall Street Crash. She was killed in a car crash in the Jim Crow South. Even her death was memorable and, sadly, beautifully timed. It is arguable that she might not have been so incredibly influential had she not died at precisely that moment in time.

*A long time ago, far away from the Tennessee River and the small ramshackle cabin, lived a woman who married a greedy man. The woman was actually Queen of the Blues. The man's name was Jack Gee. Now Jack Gee knew his Queen could make him a lot of money and money was the thing that made that fellow happy. He could sit stroking it and counting it all through the night and into the morning. One day the fellow Jack Gee discovered that another man, by the name of Clarence Williams, was stealing his wife's money. Well, at daybreak he and his Queen went off to the city to see the man who had stolen his Queen's money.*

*The thief was the man who played the piano while his Queen sang the blues. That man had signed a piece of paper that gave him half of the Queen's earnings. He made an extra three hundred and seventy-five dollars. Jack Gee had smoke coming from his nostrils he was so angry. But the Queen now, she was not a woman to mess with. She didn't need a husband to stand up for her. The minute the thief Clarence Williams sees them storm into his midtown Manhattan office, he loses his voice, loses his power of speech. The sight of Jack and his muscles and gigantic fists sent the thief crawling underneath his desk. Jack yelled,*

*'Come out of there, you dirty no-good cheating bastard' –*
*words which could have accurately described Jack himself,*
*a few years later. Williams, shaking and his bottom lip*
*trembling uncontrollably, crawled out; he looked like a*
*large soft insect. Before the two men could say boo to a*
*goose, the Queen jumped on Williams and pounded him*
*to the floor with her clenched fists. She kept on battering*
*him until Jack and she got what they wanted – a release*
*from the bit of paper that bound her to Clarence Williams.*
*But the strange thing was late that same night the Queen*
*discovered that it was not just the thief who was stealing*
*from her, but her own husband, the one that was lying there*
*sleeping in her big bed. That man could not feel a pea under*
*his sheets; but he could always tell right away if she placed*
*a dime under the mattress.*

Having been initially wary of the blues, Columbia now
knew they were on to a good thing. Bessie was selling like
pigs' feet. After they had 'sorted things out' with Clarence
Williams, Jack Gee and Bessie Smith went to see Frank
Walker at Columbia Records, who became Bessie's manager. He wrote Bessie a cheque for $500 and struck a new
deal. It guaranteed her $125 for four songs. But with-
out saying anything, Frank Walker struck out the royalty
clause. Bessie and Jack knew nothing about royalties, so
they didn't realise that Bessie was being had yet again. For
Bessie, completely unaware of the deception, $500 was
more money than she had ever dreamed of.

*Let's talk about one time. There was this woman, Bessie Smith, who was Empress of the Blues. One night the people were out lining the street waiting to hear a big concert with lots of blues singers at the New Star Casino. There was Mamie Smith, Sara Martin, Edna Hicks, Eva Taylor and Clara Smith. All of a sudden, there was a terrific commotion on the stage. Bessie threw a chair at somebody. Then she was dragged out of there by three men. She was cussing and carrying on. The three strong men had a hard job of it, dragging her across the floor. She was big and powerful. She could cuss worse than a sailor. She never did appear that night with the other blueswomen.*

*Well, first up was Mamie Smith. She tried to sing 'Crazy Blues', but the minute she opened her mouth she froze on the spot and her voice went dead. The same thing happened to Sara Martin. When Clara Smith got on, she was going to sing 'Far Away Blues' when all of a sudden she just started flying up and up and up. She went right through the roof of the New Star Casino and ended up in the sky. Some say that's her, next to the Plough, still burning bright and still claiming 'She Going Back to Where She Used Ta Be'. Now Bessie, well, she was a different matter. She made it out through the front door. Not a soul in sight. Jumped in a plush car that was waiting for somebody else. Got the driver to take her to a buffet flat. At the buffet flat she saw a woman perform tricks she wouldn't have thought humanly possible. There was one fat woman performing tricks with a lit cigarette. Now that's*

*what I call an educated pussy, Bessie thought to herself,*
*before downing a pint of good moonshine.*

The Empress often refused to share a bill with any other woman who was singing the blues. She gave this order to 'the men who ran No. 91', as Ethel Waters recalled:

> I agreed to this. I could depend a lot on my shaking, though I never shimmied vulgarly and only to express myself. And when I went on I sang 'I Want to Be Somebody's Baby Doll So I Can Get My Lovin' All the Time'. But before I could finish this number the people out front started howling, 'Blues! Blues! Come on, Stringbean, we want your blues!'
>
> Before the second show, the manager went to Bessie's dressing room and told her he was going to revoke the order forbidding me to sing any blues . . . There was quite a stormy discussion about this, and you could hear Bessie yelling things about 'these northern bitches'. Now nobody could have taken the place of Bessie Smith.[41]

What did the acknowledged 'Empress of the Blues' have to fear from any other woman singing the blues? There was no other voice like hers. Other blueswomen have often said so. 'Nobody could sing the blues like Bessie,' admitted May Wright Johnson, while being sure to tell us: 'She wasn't a friend, mind you. She would come round to the house. But she was very rough.'[42] So why did she refuse? Perhaps it was nothing to do with insecurity, or feeling threatened, or competitiveness; perhaps the sound of others singing the blues before she was ready to go on simply put her off her own work. Perhaps she knew she was unique and wanted her talent to be taken seriously, or perhaps she just had a huge ego and didn't like the idea of anybody else being celebrated for the kind of songs that she regarded as her own. Perhaps she thought, 'I am the greatest.' It is interesting there has been so much disapproval of Bessie Smith for her reaction to other blues singers; in fact, she had good friendships with most of them, had a good laugh with Ma Rainey whenever they met up, affectionately called Ethel Waters 'Long Goody', and recorded songs with Clara Smith. She was happy to be friendly with her so-called 'rivals'. I don't believe she saw them as rivals at all. I think she knew her own talent and did not want it compromised, or the impact of it weakened by having other blues on the same bill.

There are many tales about Bessie's generosity. If she were around today, she would probably be labelled a shopaholic, a binge-buyer, addicted to giving people gifts. She bought cars for Jack on impulse. She would just need to see him looking adoringly at a car, and she'd buy it, even if she was told it was a showpiece Cadillac and not intended for sale. She paid $5,000 for that Cadillac in cash. A lot of money in the 1920s. She was almost as generous to her sisters, buying them a house and giving them an allowance. But what was she really trying to buy and why did she have to buy expensive gifts for people so often? It is easy to see why Bessie Smith spent her money like she did, with no mentality of 'saving up for a rainy day'. The way she spent her money mirrored her own personality. She liked to put her hand down. Money just became another expression of her impulsive, party-loving, binge-drinking generosity. Her attitude to money wasn't any different to her attitude to sex. If she liked something, she bought it. If she wanted somebody, man or woman, she had them. She was totally free in this sense, completely uninhibited, and never once stopped indulging her own desires. I suppose you could call her hedonistic. But when you consider her background and the poverty that she came from, you can understand why she so enjoyed showering people with gifts, why it was so important to her to spend so much on her family. I can picture her, lying on her bed, awake at night, dreaming about what she was going to buy her family. It must have been like a childhood wish come true. Lying awake on a bed with lovely soft, clean sheets, in a house with running water, a warm house in Philadelphia, a long long way from Chattanooga, lying there dreaming about what to buy her sisters. From poor to rich, like a fairy tale. Who would have believed that one day she'd be able to buy anything she wanted. Except love, of course. She couldn't buy love. Perhaps she thought she could. Perhaps she imagined that if she bought Jack a new Cadillac he would love her like no other. She loved him for buying her that dress with the money from his pawned watch. She never forgot that moment when he arrived home with that red dress in that big paper bag. He'd got her size right and everything. She liked that dress so much she wanted to sleep in it. It was the first time in her life that anybody had ever bought her anything. Presents mean more to people who have been poor. Maybe she thought everyone would be like she was with that dress Jack bought her. But Jack and her sisters started to take her wild generosity for granted; they started to expect the gift, to wait for it and to turn sour if it didn't just magically appear as she walked through the door.

She also used her money to help friends out of trouble. When she heard an old friend, Buster Porter, a man she had worked with, was in a Cleveland hospital and unable to pay his medical bills, she grabbed a cab during one of the breaks in her show and went to him. She gave the sick entertainer $50. She bailed friends out of jail with her money. Once she had to rescue Ma Rainey, who had found herself in a compromising position with the Chicago police. She'd been having a wild party with a group of young women; the party got so noisy that a neighbour called the police. The cops arrived just as Ma and the girls were in the middle of an orgy. There was pandemonium as everyone scrambled madly for their clothes and ran out of the back door, wearing each other's knickers. Ma Rainey, clutching someone else's dress, was the last to leave by the back exit. But she fell down the stairs. The police caught her, accused her of running an indecent party and threw her in jail. Bessie, who must have been more than sympathetic to

Ma's predicament, having run many such parties herself, bailed Ma out the following morning.

The party life was never better than in the Harlem of the 1920s. It could be said that home entertainment never had it so good. These parties were known as 'rent parties' or parlor socials. You could get into one for anything from ten cents to a dollar. The other guests were ordinary, working-class people: tradesmen, housemaids, laundry workers, seamstresses, porters, elevator 'boys'. But writers and artists and singers loved to go along too. On a Saturday night in Harlem, the music pounded out of the open windows. There was always an upright piano, a guitar, a trumpet and sometimes a snare drum. Rent parties originated in the South, where rents were so high that people had to organise such socials to pay their landlords. You needed no social standing to throw a rent party. All you needed was a piano player and a few dancing girls. Jervis Anderson describes a typical rent party:

Drinks were bathtub gin and whiskey. Food was fried fish, chicken, corn bread, rice and beans, chitterlings, potato salad, pigs' feet. 'Whist' games were actually poker and dice. Music, in the parlance of the day, was 'gut bucket', played by some of the masters and students of Harlem stride piano. Dancing – the Charleston, the black bottom, the monkey hunch, the mess around, the shimmy, the bo-hog, the camel, the skate and the buzzard – went on till the break of day . . .

135

You were not regarded as much of a jazz pianist unless, wherever else you appeared, you played the rent-party circuit. You earned your spurs not only by sending the dancers into flights of ecstasy but also by 'cutting,' or outperforming, rival piano players.[43]

Duke Ellington, Bill Basie – not yet Count – a young Fats Waller and Bessie Smith enjoyed these rent parties. Fats was already fat and playing the piano like nobody else. Count Basie remembers Fats at those parties. He was a daily customer, 'hanging on to his every note, sitting behind him all the time, enthralled by the ease with which his hands pounded the keys and his feet manipulated the pedals'. Did Bessie get into them chitterling struts or was she too interested in the pigs' feet and the seamstresses? Some of those piano battles lasted five hours; by then the Empress would be out of her head on bathtub gin, not giving a damn for the boys' 'carving battles'.

One of Bessie's best-known songs, 'Gimme a Pigfoot', written by Leola 'Coot' Grant and Wesley Wilson and performed with Jack Teagarden and Benny Goodman in 1933, is about rent parties:

Up in Harlem ev'ry Saturday night
When the high brows git together it just too tight.
They all congregates at an all-night strut
And what they do is tut-tut-tut.
Old Hannah Brown from 'cross town

Gets full of corn and starts breakin' 'em down.
Just at the break of day
You can hear old Hannah say –
Gimme a pigfoot and a bottle of beer,
Send me again, I don't care.
I feel just like I want to clown,
Give the piano player a drink because he's bringing me
    down.
He's got rhythm, yeah, when he stomps his feet
He sends me – right off to sleep.

The last lines of this Harlem party song sum Bessie up
– 'Slay me 'cause I'm in my sin, / Slay me 'cause I'm full
of gin.' The gutsy way she sings that 'yeah' is like nobody
else. She drags that *yeah* out of herself. She knew how to
let herself go; didn't give a damn what anyone thought of
her. She knew how to give herself up to the mood: 'Send
me 'cause I don't care, / Slay me 'cause I don't care . . .'
Drunk and full of the high of that strutting piano, the
place Bessie was sent to was more wonderful than any
other. It was free of Jack, free of the pressure to record
or perform herself, she could completely lose herself at
those parties. And Bessie did want to lose herself. Jack was
very judgemental of her going to or throwing any type of
party. If he caught her partying, he'd beat her. The parties
were an escape from Jack; they were also forbidden fruit,
or forbidden pigs' feet.

*Say that the Empress went out one night to the house of a man called Carl Van Vechten. Say it was a nice house, a smart house. Say he had a pretty wife. Now Carl Van Vechten was one of Bessie's many white admirers. He was rich and he was a journalist whose interest was the black writers and musicians of the Harlem Renaissance. There was no time like the twenties in Harlem if you liked to have fun. Van Vechten held parties that were a bit different from the rent parties; at his parties, you could meet the New York cultural elite. 'Dicty blacks' that Bessie loathed. They didn't like her either. That woman knew crude language inside out. She could cuss up a storm. She could make clouds in the sky appear dark and heavy with her bad language. The rain could pour down and it still couldn't put out her tongue. She wasn't scared of nothing, least of all cussing. She was never quiet awhile. She just came right out and said what she thought. No, those well-to-do blacks believed the Empress swearing reflected badly on them. Alone, they could hold up a mirror to themselves and see the wild face of that roaring violent woman staring right back. It frightened them to think they and she could be connected in any way. She was the same colour. 'That woman is bad for the race,' they said and walked away.*

*Heard tell about 1928. The Empress arrives with Porter Grainger, the composer of her current show,* Mississippi Days, *dressed up to the nines in ermine and dripping with jewels. Right aways she realises she is on alien territory. There's a whole sea of white faces staring at her and the*

*polite white handshake of Van Vechten is no comfort. She is*
*out of her depth, and she sure as hell is not going to drown.*
*Whenever the Empress is out of her own territory, she*
*defends herself with her own aggression. Van Vechten offers*
*her a martini; she demands a whiskey. She tells Ruby, at*
*her side at all times, to pull her damn mink coat off. Van*
*Vechten, of course, wants her to sing in his own home. He's*
*got Grainger and he's got a piano and he's got the New*
*York elite. What more could a man like Van Vechten, who*
*published a novel in 1926 entitled* Nigger Heaven, *want?*
*Now that was a dream come true. As soon as Bessie sings*
*her blues, after downing practically a pint of whiskey, she*
*is back to herself. Only music and drink can bring herself*
*back. The white faces in Carl Van Vechten's chic apartment*
*light up. Polite society can still enjoy 'Jail House Blues',*
*'Sorrowful Blues' and 'Bleeding Hearted Blues'. The*
*sadder the song, the better the hit. They could shake their*
*sad white heads when Bessie sang 'St Louis Blues'. Here*
*was somebody from the heart of the poor black community*
*dressed up in furs, drinking whiskey in between blues,*
*and singing her whole black heart off. They were moved.*
*This was a real experience. Polite society drank a bit*
*more than usual that night. Not pint measures, mind you.*
*Not whiskey. Martinis all the way through 'I Ain't Got*
*Nobody'.*

I ain't got nobody, nobody,
Nobody cares for me.

That's why I'm awfully sad and lonely,
Won't some good man take a chance with me?
I'll sing good songs, all the time,
Want some gal to be a pal of mine.
I ain't got nobody, nobody
Ain't nobody cares for me.

*As Bessie goes to leave the tiny wife of Carl Van Vechten says, 'You're not leaving without kissing me goodbye,' and leans forward to kiss her. Bessie doesn't even think. She's got fists for words like these. She knocks the small woman down, saying, 'Get the fuck away from me! I ain't never heard of such shit.' Polite society shook its small white head, horrified. And who had ever seen a hostess knocked down like that before at such a do? Van Vechten helped his wife up and escorted Bessie to the elevator. The patron of black arts went back into his room and wiped his brow with a big white handkerchief. Then he said to his company, 'Well, that's the blues for you.' His tiny wife jumped up and down on his feet. 'I'll give you the blues,' she said. At which point, polite society left. There was a queue of them waiting at that same elevator. Well, the elevator boy had a laugh that night. He laughed and laughed and laughed.*

The story of Van Vechten's party is told more than any other story about Bessie. Outside of the time and place, it is perhaps difficult to imagine the enormous impact a black woman knocking down a white woman (and rich white, too) would have had. But Bessie had no real sense of her own danger or the consequences of her violent, thoughtless actions. She just loathed being patronised by white people. She hated it when any member of her travelling troupe, from her boys in the band to the prop boys and chorines, sucked up to white people. She never did. Perhaps she just couldn't stomach the contradictions of finding herself at such an elitist soirée, and the only way to resolve the conflict was to behave completely differently from anyone else there so that she need never fear being like 'one of them'. Or perhaps she didn't think about it at all.

Bessie Smith did make a habit of reacting swiftly to anything that annoyed her with her fists. Violence and she were no strangers. Jack beat her up and she beat up other people. Anybody, from a chorine in her show, to a piano player like Clarence Williams, to Carl Van Vechten's wife, if they upset Bessie, could receive blows just about anywhere on their body. Why did she respond with violence so often? She never used words to fight. She had a fearsome temper and when she got riled there was no cooling her down. When she was wild she hated words. Only the action of fists could do. She was completely out of control. Once, having heard that Jack was unfaithful to her, she tried to shoot him from a moving train. There are countless tales about the violence of the Empress, but none actually enlighten us as to what was going on inside her mind. The point about violent people when they lose their temper is that they don't have any mind. Whether she thought about her own violence afterwards is not known either. But she always used her fists. The blues she sang also contained lots of violence: 'St Louis Gal, I'm going to hammer you, I mean manhammer you [*sic*].' In that song, she wants to beat up the woman that has stolen her man, which again anticipated real life when she beat up Gertrude Saunders for stealing Jack Gee.

Sometimes her resort to fisticuffs was admirable. Like the time when she fought off the Ku Klux Klan single-handedly. This was the twentieth-century Klan, organised in 1915 by 'Colonel' William J. Simmons, a preacher and promoter of fraternal orders. The Klan was fuelled by patriotism and a romantic nostalgia for the old South. In the 1920s its membership exceeded four million nationally. Profits rolled in from the sale of its regalia. A burning cross became its symbol. White-robed Klansmen participated in marches, parades and night-time cross burnings all over the country. Bombings, shootings, whippings and lynchings were carried out in secret. The Klan exercised a reign of terror over Southern black people. But Bessie Smith was not cowed even by the Ku Klux Klan.

*Now here it is. It was a hot day that's just cooled down. The moon is way up in the sky. The tents are up for the blues. People have arrived from all over on mules, trains, in cars, wagons. They have come to hear the woman they have been playing on their phonographs. The one who can tell it like it is. The one who speaks their own tongue. On the way to the tent, past the train station, they have*

*caught a glimpse of her famed train, bright as the yellow*
*sun was in the sky, with its great green letters. That train*
*is something. They are not arriving in quite that style. But*
*they have picnics with them. Enough food and drink to feed*
*the blues. Chicken legs. Pigs' feet. Cornbread. Tomatoes.*
*It is July 1927 in Concord, North Carolina. The whole*
*tent is buzzing and it's hard to find a place to sit down. It's*
*difficult to see where one person ends and another begins.*
*The excitement is making the canvas flap back and forth*
*even though there is no wind. The big pole in the middle*
*of the tent looks unsteady. Some folks have bought drinks*
*from the Empress's vendor. Crackerjacks. The moment*
*finally comes. The one they have journeyed all the miles*
*for. The single opening moment when that voice breaks out*
*like an animal in heat. The Empress just howls them blues*
*out. She starts off with 'Florida Bound Blues'.*

I got a letter from my daddy,
He bought me a sweet piece of land;
I got a letter from my daddy,
He bought me a small piece of ground;
You can't blame me for leavin', Lawd,
I'm Florida bound.

*Then she goes on to strut her stuff, when one of her*
*musicians, overhot, goes out and finds a bunch of hooded*
*men about to drop her tent. The sight of them in their white*
*robes makes the musician dizzy. They've already pulled*

*up several stakes. He rushes back and warns the Empress.
The Queen commands her prop boys to follow her round
the tent. She doesn't tell them why. So when they see the
Klansmen they make a speedy retreat. The Empress, on
her own, confronts the Klansmen: 'I'll get the whole damn
tent out of here if I have to. You just pick up those sheets
and run.' The Klansmen, shocked, stand and gawp whilst
the Empress shouts obscenities at them until finally they
disappear into the darkness. 'I ain't never heard of such
shit,' says the Empress, walking over to the prop boys. 'And
as for you, you ain't nothing but a bunch of sissies.' Then
she goes right back into that same tent for her encore.*

*Sorted.*

The Empress was often knocking people down or
beating them up with her own fists. But in the wild stories recounted about her, there are also some wonderful
one-liners. In Atlanta at the 81 Club in 1925, two years
after the release of her first records and at the height of her
massive popularity, the manager, Bailey, requested that all
stars go in through the back door, which was rat-infested.
But the Empress grabbed Ruby's arm and led her past the
box office into the theatre through the front door. Bailey
caught up with them just as they entered the auditor-
ium. 'If they see you before the show, they won't find you
as interesting,' he said. 'I don't give a fuck,' replied the
Empress. 'If you don't like it you can kiss my black ass and
give me my drops.'

The story of Bessie Smith is not just the story of the blues but the story of a woman who was not in control of her life. There was the constant drinking. She started drinking heavily when she was a child. Sometimes she was so drunk concerts had to be cancelled. Other times she was propped up. The speedy resort to violence probably had a lot to do with bathtub gin and white lightning. It is ironic that a lot of these violent outbursts took place in the time of Prohibition; like the time when a chorine in her show cut up the new pair of dancing shoes Bessie bought for Ruby. Bessie threatened her and she fought back, throwing a bottle across the room. Bessie asked her to go and she refused. There was one hell of a fight. The chorine ended up totally dishevelled and covered in blood. She called the police and pressed charges against Bessie. Ruby had to get the money for her bail. Bessie was often arrested by the police for her violence.

It happened again when she discovered Jack had given Gertrude Saunders some of her jewellery. She saw Gertrude in the street and knocked her unconscious. Another time, according to Albertson, Bessie spotted Gertrude out with Jack and got a hold of her. 'You motherless bitch,' she called Saunders – an interesting insult since Bessie was motherless herself – and dragged her through the mud. Gertrude screamed that she was going to get a gun and kill Bessie. 'I'll make you eat it, bitch,' was Bessie's answer, 'and every time I see you, you yellow bitch, I'm going to beat you. One of these days when you are up on stage, I'm gonna be in the audience and I'm comin' up and grabbin' you off.'[44]

Some people said Gertrude Saunders did indeed purchase a gun for defence against Bessie. Another time when Bessie attacked Gertrude she was actually given a summons.

The timing of those attacks signalled the beginning of her downward spiral. In 1929 Jack left. And by this time Bessie's recordings were only selling about eight thousand each – a far cry from the sales in 1923 of 'Gulf Coast Blues' and 'Downhearted Blues'. The Empress became a victim of the Depression; Bessie's luck was running out. In the same year she made the film *St Louis Blues*, based on W. C. Handy's song. A two-reel short. Seventeen unforgettable minutes. The only film footage in existence of the Empress. It was all about a woman suffering from an unfaithful lover. I saw it once, when I was in my teens, on the television. I remember the shock of the grainy monochrome image of my heroine appearing in this sad tale of woe. There she was, a tall, beautiful woman, driven to drink by her feckless lover. She catches her lover at it, marching through a crap game, and throws her rival out of the room. Then she herself is thrown to the floor by the faithless lover. On the floor she starts singing 'St Louis Blues':

I hate to see the evening sun go down,
I hate to see the evening sun go down,
It makes me think I'm on my last go-round.
Feeling tomorrow like I feel today,
Feeling tomorrow like I feel today,
I pack my grip and make my getaway.

St Louis woman with her diamond rings,
Pulls my man around by her apron strings.

The lover reappears; they embrace; he steals a wad of notes from her stocking, pushes her into the bar and struts out the place. He could have been Jack Gee.

Ironically enough, 'St Louis Blues' was turned down by every major Tin Pan Alley publisher. W. C. Handy had to set up his own publishing company to issue the song. 'It did not become popular for years, until vaudeville and revue singers began using it in their acts.'[45]

It is impossible to know how many of the stories of Bessie Smith's violence are true, and how many are made up, or embellished and exaggerated out of all proportion. Gertrude Saunders, years later, maintained that she and Bessie had never come to blows, and that she felt sorry for Bessie because her love of Jack was so intense and yet Jack treated her so badly. Today her so-called binge-drinking or heavy drinking would simply be called alcoholism, and all her wild, tempestuous behaviour would be explained by that addiction. Her terrible mood swings, her violence, her insecurity, her bad language, the fact that she never went anywhere without corn liquor in her purse, all point to her being a serious alcoholic. Why did she need to drink so much? The stories are good crack, but she was out of control. She was running. She frequently drank herself unconscious and woke up to beat people up. She can't have felt all that good about herself. After her violent outbursts, she probably felt remorse. Who knows? Maybe she felt justified. Maybe she felt whoever it was that was receiving her blows at any given time deserved it. Maybe she didn't think about violence at all. She just let rip and then it was over until the next time.

That there are almost as many stories about Bessie Smith's violent, drunken bawdiness as there are blues is interesting in itself. It is not just her blues that fascinate, but her wild, drunk, promiscuous, generous, cussing personality. The legends and myths of the Empress will live on as long as the blues survive. Whether they are true or not. 'All stories are true.'

Preach 'em blues, sing 'em blues,
Moan 'em blues, holler 'em blues,
Let me convert your soul.
Sing 'em, sing 'em, sing them blues,
Let me convert your soul.

'Preachin' the Blues'

# THE BLUES

It was the real thing: A wonderful heart cut open
with a knife until it was exposed for all to see.

Carl Van Vechten

Whatever Bessie Smith sang automatically became
a blues.

Paul Garon

Whatever pathos there is in the world, whatever
sadness she had, was brought out in singing – and
the audience knew it and responded to it.

Frank Schiffman

Bessie Smith's blues tell the story of her life better than
biography or autobiography ever could. Bessie Smith's
life and her blues are as opposite sides of the same coin.
Many weirdly anticipated events in her life. She sang
'Nobody Knows You When You're Down and Out' before
the Depression hit her and her friends started to leave her.
'Jail House Blues' she sang in 1923, before she'd ever been
arrested for any violence. The lyrics probably came right
back to her though, when she was in jail for real. 'Good
morning blues, blues, how do you do, / Say I've just come
here to have a few words with you.' She was not singing

about some distant imaginary character. Even when she didn't know it yet, it turned out she was singing about herself. Her blues are autobiography. They favoured almost exclusively the first-person narrative. She is so intimate with her lyrics because she knows what they are saying. She knows her life. The key to understanding the complex personality of Bessie Smith is all in her blues.

'Baby Doll', 'Backwater Blues', 'Blue Blues', 'Death Valley Moan', 'Dirty No-Gooder Blues', 'Dixie Flyer Blues', 'Don't Fish in My Sea', 'Foolish Man Blues', 'Golden Rule Blues', 'Hard Time Blues', 'He's Gone Blues', 'Hot Springs Blues', 'In the House Blues', 'It Makes My Love Come Down', 'Jail House Blues', 'Jot 'Em Down Blues', 'Lonesome Desert Blues', 'Long Old Road', 'Lost Your Head Blues', 'My Man Blues', 'Pickpocket Blues', 'Pinchbacks, Take 'Em Away', 'Please Help Me Get Him Off My Mind', 'Poor Man's Blues', 'Reckless Blues', 'Rocking Chair Blues', 'Safety Mama', 'Shipwreck Blues', 'Soft Pedal Blues', 'Sorrowful Blues', 'Spider Man Blues', 'Standin' in the Rain Blues', 'Sweet Potato Blues', 'Telephone Blues', 'Thinking Blues', 'Wasted Life Blues', 'Young Woman's Blues'.

These are just the ones she wrote herself. Some of them uniquely capture specific moments in her life. Jack's nervous breakdowns in 'Hot Springs Blues'. Her own reaction to the postwar boom that favoured white people is in 'Poor Man's Blues':

> Now the war is over, all man must live the same as you;
> Now the war is over, all man must live the same as you;
> If it wasn't for the poor man, Mister Rich Man, what
> would you do?

'Backwater Blues' is an example of her writing a blues herself to reflect the experience of ordinary working–class people. She went to a small town near Cincinnati which was flooded. She had to step off the train into a little row-boat. Her audience shouted for her to sing 'Backwater Blues', but this was a song she did not know. Perhaps they were suggesting she should write it. 'Backwater Blues' is one of her most powerful compositions, probably because it came out of this strange experience, and because there was a demand for a song that did not yet exist. She record-ed it on 17 February 1927 with James P. Johnson.

> I woke up this mornin', can't even get out of my do';
> I woke up this mornin', can't even get out of my do';
> There's enough trouble to make a poor girl wonder
> where she wanna go . . .
> Backwater blues done caused me to pack my things and
> go;
> Backwater blues done caused me to pack my things and
> go;

'Cause my house fell down, and I can't live there no
    mo'.

The blues she sang and the blues she wrote often contained elements of burlesque, music hall and vaudeville
which reflected her background as a young girl who had
first joined a travelling troupe in 1912. A lot of her blues
were raunchy, bawdy, double-entendre-filled, sexy songs,
as well as tragic, painful and depressing. As W. C. Handy
put it:

> The blues came from the man farthest down. The blues
> came from nothingness, from want, from desire. And
> when a man sang or played the blues, a small part of the
> want was satisfied from the music. The blues go back to
> slavery, to longing. My father, who was a preacher, used
> to cry every time he heard someone sing, 'I'll See You
> on Judgement Day.' When I asked him why, he said,
> 'That's the song they sang when your uncle was sold
> into slavery in Arkansas. He wouldn't let his masters
> beat him, so they got rid of him the way they would a
> mule.'[46]

Bessie's blues moved people. Her voice just got to them.
Perhaps she reminded them of the past, of losses, of longing. Something in her voice went way back into a deeper
past. Her voice seemed to contain history, tragedy, slavery, without self-pity. It had the ability to stretch beyond

even the lyrics of her blues into something more complex. Her blues were universal, but also deeply personal. They allowed her to express the whole range of her complex personality: the wild promiscuous drunken side ('T'ain't Nobody's Business', 'Gimme a Pigfoot', 'It Makes My Love Come Down', 'He's Got Me Goin', 'Young Woman's Blues') and the depressed, insecure, lonely side ('I've Been Mistreated and I Don't Like It', 'Nobody Knows You', 'Wasted Life Blues', 'Baby Won't You Please Come Home', 'Empty Bed Blues').

Relationships, principally relationships with men, are the key troubles in her blues. Not poverty, not poor health, not alcoholism, not floods, not death, not gambling – although she did write and sing blues about all these subjects. As Albert Murray points out:

> In fact in the 160 available recordings of Bessie
> Smith . . . the preoccupation is clearly not all with hard
> workmasters, cruel sheriffs, biased prosecutors, juries
> and judges, but with the careless love of aggravating
> papas, sweet mistreaters, dirty no-gooders, and spider
> men.[47]

Spider men. They sound awful. She wrote 'Spider Man Blues' herself too. In some of her blues, she begs for the man to change himself, plaintively; and in others she states she's had enough. She's not putting up with it any more. 'I Ain't Gonna Play No Second Fiddle', 'Safety Mama'. Her songs do not reflect the fact that she had just as much sex with women. There is no reason to presume, however, that every character she sings about is actually a man. When she sings songs like 'Empty Bed Blues', she could be missing a woman just as easily as a man.

The men in her life, principally Jack Gee and Earl Love, her two unsuccessful husbands, as well as the men she had relationships with on the road, consistently let her down; she did not believe that a good man could exist. Her blues reflect this. 'Dirty No-Gooder Blues', 'Foolish Man Blues', 'My Man Blues', 'Spider Man Blues', 'Please Help Me Get Him off My Mind'. Not just one man, but all men are bastards as far as these songs go. They are not just bastards, they are bad for you. Men, in Bessie's blues, destroy and ruin women, they waste their lives; in order for a woman to survive she needs to get away from men. She needs to stand up to them, to not take any more of it, and to get on a train to Chicago. 'I'm a good ole gal but I've just been treated wrong' ('Lost Your Head Blues').

There are times when she puts up with it:

I swear I won't call no copper
If I'm beat up by my papa.
T'ain't nobody's business if I do.
                    'T'ain't Nobody's Business'

But these lines are in direct contrast to:

I've been mistreated and I don't like it,
There's no use to say I do.

'I've Been Mistreated and I Don't Like It'

Or these:

Daddy, Mama's got the blues
The kind of blues that's hard to lose
'Cause you mistreated me
And drove me from your door . . .
Mistreating Daddy, mistreating Mama all the time . . .
Mistreating Daddy, Mama's crossed the danger line.

'Mistreating Daddy'

The songs she wrote herself about men are much more revealing. The lines are more direct and the pain cuts deeper:

Lord, I wish I could die because my man treats me like a
    slave,
Lord, I wish I could die my man treats me like a slave.
As to why he drives me, I'm sinking low, low in my
    grave.
He's a hard drivin' papa, drive me all the time,
Drives me so hard I'm afraid that I'll lose my mind. . .
And when the sun starts sinking, I start sinking into
    crime.

He takes all my money and starts to cry for more.
I'm goin' to the river feelin' so sad and blue,

I'm goin' to the river feelin' so sad and blue,
Because I love him 'cause there's no one can beat me
   like he do.

                              'Hard Drivin' Papa'


Bessie's 'Hard Drivin' Papa', was first recorded on 4 May 1926. Six months later, she's still writing about a man who wants her money in 'Lost Your Head Blues': 'I was with you baby when you didn't have a dime.' Jack Gee obviously features highly in her own songs. She was sorely let down by him. 'Since you got money, it's done changed your mind.' She wrote this song three years before she actually left him: 'I'm gonna leave baby, ain't gonna say goodbye.' Once again, the blues saw into her future. Jack Gee couldn't handle having money. It totally corrupted him; he was no longer the nice man who had been shot on a date, but a money-grabbing chancer. The fact that his behaviour made the Empress suicidal is obvious in her blues. 'I'm going to the river, feeling so sad and blue.'

Bessie Smith's blues show how perceptive she was about people and herself, about her own complicity. They also reveal a fear of losing herself, that a man can drive her so hard, 'I'm afraid that I'll lose my mind.' But even worse than losing her mind is the death wish at the beginning of the song. 'Lord, I wish I could die because my man treats me like a slave.' Addressed to the Lord, this blues is like a plea to get out of life, to be free. 'Treats me like a slave' would have been a more shocking line then than it is now for African-American people hadn't been out of slavery for all that long. The man in this song gives her no freedom; there is no escape; no respect; no autonomy. Just like the girl in 'Backwater Blues', 'There ain't no place for a poor old girl to go.' There is a pervasive sense of Bessie being totally trapped in her destructive relationships with men. There she was, with more money than any black woman in the country, making her own records, writing her own songs, yet still being battered by her talentless husband. It really says something about the power of sexism. The Empress is 'treated like a slave'.

It is this complexity that beats at the heart of Bessie Smith's personality. The woman who didn't take any rubbish from anybody, who cussed and beat up many people, and the woman who was beaten herself, who had her money stolen and was humiliated by her husband. No matter how rich or famous she became, she never resolved that contradiction. She was never totally in control of it. There is the sweet man and there is the sour man. 'I fell in love with a sweet man once, he said he loved me too.' Then there are the men who are both, the sweet mistreaters. Her blues never offer resolutions. They explore conflicts but they don't resolve anything. Like good stories, they let you enter with your imagination and participate in the conflict. Nothing is pat or finished, except jelly rolls, as Will Friedwald states:

Smith also encompassed a tantalizing mixture of what was past and what was to come . . . With Smith, the two seemingly incongruous attitudes are compatible, a sort of tender invective. Smith sings about love without a trace of sentiment, and of sex without guilt. She has an amazingly realistic attitude toward life and love . . . devoid of self-pity. As far as jazz, blues and popular music are concerned, Smith was the first fully three-dimensional recording artist, the first to use the new medium to express a complete personality.[48]

There is so much sauce in her blues as well, so much feisty cheek and humour. One of my early favourites, 'Kitchen Man', is a wonderful example. It was written by Andreamenentania Paul Razafinkeriefo (Andy Razaf), who was the nephew of Queen Ranavalona III of Madagascar. He also wrote, with Fats Waller, 'Honeysuckle Rose' and 'Ain't Misbehavin'. The double entendres in 'Kitchen Man' are practically pornographic, though I didn't really understand them back then. Often Bessie Smith deviated from the words written down, probably because some of them were unfamiliar. In 'Kitchen Man' she sings 'foor men' for 'footmen', which suggests she hadn't heard of a footman.

I love his cabbage gravy, his hash . . .
I can't do without my kitchen man . . .

Like the way he warms my chops,
I can't do without my kitchen man . . .

Oh his jelly roll is so nice and hot,

Never fails to touch the spot,
I can't do without my kitchen man.

His frankfurters are oh so sweet,
How I like his sausage meat,
I can't do without my kitchen man.

Oh how that boy can open clams,
No one else can touch my hams,
I can't do without my kitchen man.

When I eat his doughnuts,
All I leave is the hole
Anytime he wants to,
Why, he can use my sugar bowl . . .

Only when food is mentioned in Bessie Smith's blues
are sexual relationships with men any fun – raunchy, lowdown, wild-about-that-thing fun. The rest is a bum ride.
Doughnuts and jelly rolls, clams and hams aside, what she
sings most about is a lack of love. The majority of Bessie's
blues are about looking for love. Love is something she is
constantly searching for, but never quite finds: 'I wanna be
somebody's baby doll / So I can get my lovin' all the time.'
She is desperate for love. Possibly, her mother dying when
she was so young intensified this quest for love. When she
wrote 'Reckless Blues' in 1925 her mother had already
been dead for twenty-three years. Despite her powerful
looks, there is a perception of herself in her own songs

as unattractive. No wonder, with impresarios turning her down for being 'too dark'. In her blues, she believes other women are beautiful, but she still deserves love.

When I wasn't nothing but a child,
When I wasn't nothing but a child,
All you men tried to drive me wild.

Now, I am growing old,
Now, I am growing old,
And I got what it takes to get all of you men told.

My mama says I'm reckless, my daddy says I'm wild.
My mama says I'm reckless, my daddy says I'm wild.
I ain't good-lookin' but I'm somebody's angel child.

Daddy, Mama wants some loving,
Daddy, Mama wants some loving,
Hurry pretty Papa, Mama wants some lovin' right now.

'Reckless Blues'

The line 'I ain't good-lookin' but I'm somebody's angel child' is wishful thinking because both her parents were long dead. If her mother were still alive, how much she would have been loved. Maybe the line 'Mama wants some loving' is ambiguous and she is actually talking about wanting love from her mother. She wrote this song when she was thirty-one. Already she had a sense of getting older. The song looks back at herself when she was younger. The way she hangs on to the 'now' for so long in 'Now [beat, beat, beat], I am growing old' is extraordinary.

Although the main issue in her blues is love and lack of love, a significant number of her songs were about social issues, crime and punishment, poverty and ill health, work and death. Some of the blues she sang that are less well known, and not included in any of the more recent compilations are: 'Send Me to the 'Lectric Chair', 'Homeless Blues', 'Jail House Blues', 'Sing-Sing Prison Blues', 'Work House Blues' and 'House Rent Blues'. The woman in 'Send Me to the 'Lectric Chair' asks the judge to hear her plea, but doesn't want any sympathy because she has slit her good man's throat. Then she actually asks to be sent to the electric chair, wanting to take a journey to the devil down below: 'I just killed my man, I want to reap what I sow, / Judge, Judge, hear me Judge, send me to the 'lectric chair.' She tells the judge how she sat laughing round her man whilst he was dying. The combination of the extraordinary plea with the graphically violent descriptions of the murder makes the song wildly funny. I can imagine women hearing it in 1927 and splitting their sides laughing. The music is humorous in the background: Joe Smith on witty cornet, Charlie Green on trombone. The trombone after each 'Judge, Judge', is critically timed.

I imagine her sitting down and composing her blues, sitting down because in every photograph but one that I have ever seen of Bessie Smith, she is standing up, performing. I imagine her at her kitchen table singing the words to herself till they sound right, then memorising them. She was not very literate; she'd get out a pencil and write down what she could but her memory was a necessity. She learned all 160 songs that she sang off by heart, so that when she went into the recording studio she would not slip up. She'd sing her life to herself while cooking and stirring, humming the melody till it sounded as good as the stew tasted. I imagine her trying out her new blues on Ruby. 'Ruby, what do you think of this?' and Ruby maybe making one or two adjustments. I like to see the two of them laughing at those lines, 'There's nineteen men living in my neighbourhood, / Eighteen of them are fools and the one ain't no doggone good.' Ruby saying, 'That's definitely a hit!' and pouring Bessie some homebrewed lethal concoction. Did she enjoy creating blues lyrics and compositions as much as singing them, or more? They were surely her way of working herself out, her way of exploring her own contradictions and making sense of herself. Her blues are littered with clues about how she saw herself and what she thought of herself and also how she saw the world. Luck changes, turns your life upside down. This sense of bad luck, of sudden things happening and changing your fortune, is everywhere in her blues, like a sixth sense.

'Thinking Blues', which she wrote in 1928, begins with a woman thinking about someone who has been 'nice and kind' when a letter comes from an old lover giving her the blues so bad. 'Don't you hear me baby, knocking on your door, / Have you got the nerve to drive me from your door?'

The man begs to be taken back and tries one more time. She replies, 'The good book says you've got to reap what you sow.' Again the song doesn't offer a resolution, it just explores the problem of whether or not a woman should take a man back after he has betrayed her. 'Hard Time Blues', which she wrote in 1926, also explores the dilemma of a woman who has been abandoned by her man. In this song the woman is packing her bags and leaving town.

My man says he didn't want me,
I'm getting tired of his dirty ways.
I'm going to see another brown,
I'm packing my clothes, I'm leaving town . . .

But when the good woman is gone, hard times will strike at the man and cut him down to size. Many of her blues reveal this glorious desire for revenge, even invoking the weather on her side. That man is going to get his comeuppance: 'The rising sun ain't gonna set in the east no more.' The revenge continues till it ends up with the man 'Down on your knees you'll ask for me.' Her blues are not just about being mistreated; they also detail an attempt to take control over her life. It is the man who gives the woman the blues in the first place – 'I've got the blues and it's all about my honey man' – but after that it's up to the woman to get out of it, even if that means escaping by dying – 'I'd rather be in the ocean . . . than to stay with him and be mistreated like a dog.' ('Honey Man Blues', 1926). Or, in 'Rocking

Chair Blues' (1924), she sings: 'I won't be back until you change your ways / I'm going to the river, carrying a brand new rocking chair.'

She recorded 'Black Mountain Blues' (not to be confused with 'Red Mountain Blues', altogether a happier affair) in 1930, with cornettist Ed Allen, who also played for her in 'Nobody Knows You'. 'Black Mountain' becomes synonymous with the Depression. It is a rough and ready place where there are no laws and everybody is out for themselves: 'Back in Black Mountain, a child will smack your face, / Babies crying for liquor and all the birds sing bass.' Bessie was on the long road down; she was making $500 per week now as opposed to her former $2,000. Ma Rainey wasn't doing too well either in her show *Bandanna Babies*. The audiences of the South still loved the Empress and gave her a warm welcome whenever she returned. But the South was not enough. She didn't stop being generous though and still bought presents for everybody.

On 20 November 1931, Columbia dropped the Empress. Bessie had recorded with Columbia for over nine years and had been almost single-handedly responsible for Columbia's rise to fame. The last two songs Bessie recorded for them on that date were 'Safety Mama' and 'Need a Little Sugar in My Bowl' – the latter would go on to be sung by many jazz singers, most memorably by Nina Simone years later. Columbia did not cut anything like the number of records they had cut in her heyday; now it was down to only four hundred. It was the decline and fall of the Empress. She became a has-been. She lived for a while off the earnings of her boyfriend, Richard Morgan, an easy-going Chicago bootlegger who was the uncle of musician Lionel Hampton. (Bootleggers prospered during the Depression. People always needed a good drink, especially if times were hard. A good moonshine could always cheer you up.) All over America talking pictures started to take over from theatre shows, and the vaudeville theatres closed. Ethel Waters made it in France; but Bessie Smith never left America, never reached out to a wider European audience. Had she survived, Bessie might have succeeded in the way that Ethel Waters or Alberta Hunter did.

In 1933 she recorded some songs for Okeh Records, who had turned her down ten years before. Here she was in good company, with Jack Teagarden and Buck Washington, who recorded some of her most famous songs: 'Do Your Duty', 'Gimme a Pigfoot', 'Down in the Dumps' and 'Take Me for a Buggy Ride'. 'Down in the Dumps' turned out to be the Empress's swansong. It is the only time you can hear her with swing accompaniment. Later both Billie Holiday in the 1940s and Nina Simone in the 1960s went on to sing 'Gimme a Pigfoot', although both omitted the references to reefers and marijuana that are in Bessie's version. Billie Holiday shared that same troubling quality that Bessie Smith had. According to Johnny Mercer, 'There was something about her – not just the torchy quality of her voice – that made you want to try to help her.'[49]

In 1935, Bessie appeared at the Apollo Theatre in

Harlem, owned by Frank Schiffman, who tried to persuade her to change her chorus girls because their skin was too dark and they looked gray. Bessie, however, demanded amber lights. 'If you don't want my girls, you don't want me . . . I don't give a damn, because I'm tired of wearing myself out. I can go home, get drunk, and be a lady – it's up to you.'[50] Bessie won the battle of the dark-skin girls; a little *coup d'état* of her career, possibly remembering that time in 1912 when she was thrown out of Irving C. Miller's chorus line for not being a 'glorious brownskin girl'. Ruby said, 'You never saw people give applause like they did for us girls – we broke it up!'

Two weeks earlier, Billie Holiday had made her Apollo debut. And people were already talking about the young Ella Fitzgerald. Bessie had stars on her back and she had to fight to maintain her own reputation. Luckily for Bessie, in 1936 Billie came down with a case of ptomaine poisoning and had to leave her show. Bessie Smith substituted for her. That night in 1936 at Connie's Inn helped Bessie get back on her feet again. She reached out to a wider audience. Around this time, she chummed up with Mildred Bailey. They both shared the camaraderie of fat, with routine jokes to each other about size. When they met, they would both say, 'Look I got this brand-new dress, but it's too big for me, so why don't you take it?'[51]

During this time Bessie continued to write and compose blues, although they were not recorded. Eubie Blake, a pianist and composer, remembers her coming into W. C.

Handy's office at the Apollo in April 1936 with new songs. He says they were good ideas but he was concerned that they would not make money, so they were never recorded. We will never know the lyrics of the last blues of the Empress.

Please don't let me lose my rightful mind
'Cause them is graveyard words.
                    'Them's Graveyard Words'

# MISSISSIPPI, 1937

Note: Other reports on the circumstances of this singer's death have proven incorrect.
    Sheldon Harris, *Blues Who's Who*

Someways, you could have said beforehand that there was some kind of an accident, some bad hurt coming to her. It was like she had that hurt inside her all the time, and she was just bound to find it.
    Sidney Bechet, *Treat It Gentle*

On 26 September 1937 at 11.30 a.m. in Ward One of the Afro-American Hospital, 615 Sunflower Drive, Clarksdale, Mississippi, Bessie Smith died. She had been on her way down Route 61 to a show date, travelling with Richard Morgan, with whom, for the past six years, she had been very happy. Bessie's old Packard, which Richard was driving, hit a National Biscuit Company truck parked without lights in the town of Coahoma. Her arm was virtually severed. She was still alive when she was taken to the Afro-American Hospital, where her arm was amputated, but she died hours later of shock, blood loss and internal injuries.

Her funeral was held in Philadelphia on Monday 4 October. Her body had been sent, two days earlier, by train to Philadelphia's Thirtieth Street Station, where her brother Clarence was waiting. Richard Morgan, who had survived the terrible accident, accompanied her body on the train. She was laid out at Upshur's funeral home on Twenty-first and Christian Street. When word of her death reached the black community, however, the body had to be moved to the O. V. Catto Elks Lodge on Sixteenth and Fitzwater Streets, where ten thousand mourners filed past her bier on Sunday 3 October.

Her insurance policy ensured that she had a lavish send-off the following day. Her coffin, which cost $500, was trimmed with gold and lined with pink two-tone velvet. There were forty floral arrangements. The auditorium at Catto Elks Lodge was full. The Reverend Andrew J. Sullivan presided over the service. A Mrs Emily Moten read a poem called 'Oh Life'. Somebody fainted. The crowd outside was seven thousand strong and policemen were having a hard time holding it back, just like they had in the heyday of the Empress when thousands could not get into the theatres to hear her sing the blues.

The pallbearers were hired men. They did not know Bessie. It was unusual for a dead person at a Philadelphia funeral to be carried by strangers. They walked down Sixteenth Street to the waiting hearse. A choir sang 'Rest in Peace'. The hearse did not head straight for the cemetery; it gave the Empress one last twirl round her old neighbourhood. The streets were lined with thousands of ordinary blues fans and admirers who were all devastated at the tragic death of the Empress. She was a huge star who, at the time of her death, was just beginning to make a comeback. Yet no other major stars showed up at her funeral. Ethel Waters ('Long Goody') was not there. Duke Ellington was not there. The cast of the Cotton Club Revue was not there. Louis Armstrong was not there.

It seems fitting for a woman who preferred pigs' feet parties to polite society, who never ever forgot her working-class roots, who despite her fame and fortune never changed her speech, her behaviour or her habits to conform to some notion of a star, that it was not stars and personalities who attended her funeral but ordinary people. The people who always mattered to her all along. Not the Harlem elite. All of the faces in the photographs taken of her grand exit are black. There is not a white face to be seen.

Her family attended the funeral and Richard Morgan was there. It was Jack Gee, though, who talked to reporters, claiming he had never lost touch with his wife. He later became rich on royalties paid to him from her songs. Over the years he invested in small businesses and real estate. Richard Morgan, who had been her partner for as long as Jack Gee, six years apiece, received nothing. Nor did Bessie Smith's adopted son, Jack Gee Junior.

She was buried at Mount Lawn Cemetery, Sharon Hills, Philadelphia, wearing a long silk dress that Jack Gee claimed he bought her – the second significant dress, the first being the one she wore to her first recording studio date. The newspapers said it was a farewell gift. Her family denied that he ever bought that dress and said the money from her life insurance went to pay for it.

Jack Gee, although not poor, did not buy a headstone for Bessie Smith. Nor did any of her family, despite her generosity towards them for years. It is scandalous but true that the Empress of the Blues lay in an unmarked grave until 1970. Her relatives squabbled over money. Everyone thought somebody else should be the one to pay. Bessie would probably have written a blues about that if she had been looking down from above. Her own 'Funeral Blues' or 'Nobody Bought Me a Headstone Blues'. A Bessie Smith Memorial Concert was held in Town Hall, New York City in 1948 to raise money to buy a headstone. But the stone was never bought; Maud Smith, Bessie's sister-in-law, said that Jack Gee pocketed the money. Other surviving relatives of Bessie Smith have also said that money raised from benefits was turned over to Jack Gee on at least two occasions. Chris Albertson says:

> Ruby [Walker] recalls performing at such an event in New York's Town Hall during the forties: 'Jack showed up and demanded the money. He said he'd have his lawyers stop the concert if he didn't get it. He got it, but knowing Jack he spent it on something for himself.'[52]

Maud Smith tells of another benefit held at Philadelphia's Blue Note Club in the early 1950s. She handed the cheque over to Jack and they were supposed to go and choose a stone together. But she never saw the cheque again.

The Empress of the Blues lay in an unmarked grave for thirty-three years. She was unknown at the start of her life and literally unknown in her grave. She had paid a lot of money for the insurance policy. She had wanted things to be done properly. Perhaps she knew nobody would dole out the money. Perhaps by then she knew what her family and Jack Gee were like.

What is the meaning of the unmarked grave? The graves of poor people, black and white, were not marked in the land of the brave, the home of the free. The graves of slaves were unmarked. It is like dying without a name. Like being nobody. For thirty-three years after she died, Bessie Smith was nobody. She had no name. She disappeared. She was a victim of America's epic tradition of forgetting its black people, forgetting their existence, wiping out their significance. For years the songs she sang were practically national anthems. She sang them better than anybody. ('St Louis Blues', which W. C. Handy published in 1914, became so popular during the First World War that it was said Europeans believed it to be the American national anthem.[53]) Yet the people who went to visit Bessie Smith's grave between 1937 and 1970 would have had difficulty finding it. For all those years Bessie Smith had what she probably dreaded most – a 'pauper's grave'.

It is doubtful Bessie Smith's grave would ever have been marked had it not been for the fact that in 1970, Columbia reissued her complete output on five double albums. These won two Grammy awards and the series came top in all the jazz critics' polls, winning *Billboard* magazine's 'Trendsetter of the Year Award'. The publicity generated by the release of the records prompted a black Philadelphia housewife to write a letter to the *Philadelphia Inquirer*'s Action Line, drawing attention to the unmarked grave. The *Inquirer* started to ask a number of people for donations. It took only two calls to raise the money. One offer came from Juanita Green, who used to clean Bessie's house on Saturdays when she was a wee girl. She remembers Bessie would often be singing and cooking 'chitterlings boiled with scallions, dipped in flour and fried'.[54] Juanita Green grew up to become the president of the North Philadelphia chapter of the National Association for the Advancement of Colored People (NAACP) and to own two nursing homes.

The second donor was Janis Joplin. She had always been a great admirer of Bessie Smith's and her own music was influenced by the Empress. Listen to her songs and you can hear Bessie way back in the background. 'Coming Home Blues', 'Turtle Blues', 'Kozmic Blues' and 'I Need a Man to Love' all carry the torch for the Empress. Janis Joplin also died a tragic death, in her case from a drug overdose at the Hollywood Landmark Motor Hotel in 1970. She died on 4 October, ironically the date of Bessie's funeral. Bessie would have been tickled at the combination of the two headstone donors: one, a cleaner who became owner of two nursing homes; the other, a blues singer who died a few months after donating the cash. Joplin was almost as colourful a personality as Smith herself, as *Cashbox* magazine explained: 'A mixture of Leadbelly, a steam engine, Calamity Jane, Bessie Smith, an oil derrick rot gut bourbon funneled into the 20th century somewhere between El Paso and San Francisco.'[55]

A ceremony to mark Bessie's grave was held on Friday 7 August 1970. John Hammond, who had arranged Bessie's last recording with Okeh Records, covered the gravestone with his old raincoat so that it could be unveiled. Hammond whipped the raincoat off to reveal the words: 'The Greatest Blues Singer in the World Will Never Stop Singing. Bessie Smith 1894–1937'. There was only a motley collection of about thirty people who attended the modest ceremony. Joplin, still alive at that point, was not present. It was thought that she did not want her stardom to detract from the importance of the event. Jack Gee, who was offered a taxi by Juanita Green, did not go. He cursed Juanita down the telephone instead.

Both the life *and* death of Bessie Smith have caused widespread controversy. For years following her death, it was widely believed she had been killed by the racism of Southern white hospitals refusing to admit her. As late as the 1970s people still believed this version of events to be true. Alan Lomax writes:

> They all knew there was little mercy in their
> surroundings. They had heard about what had

happened to Bessie Smith in 1937 in their hometown. Wounded in a local car wreck, the great blues singer was refused admission to three Clarksdale hospitals because she was black. In the end she bled to death without medical attention, while her friends pled with the hospital authorities to admit her. And this incident was typical of the Deep South.[56]

It *was* typical of the South. We have all heard horrible stories about the South. Sidney Bechet also believed the story. He said later, 'She was *too* far in the South.' Mahalia Jackson, the greatest gospel singer in the world, who was also influenced by Bessie Smith, wrote about the South in her autobiography, *Movin' On Up*:

> From Virginia to Florida it was a nightmare. There was no place for us to eat or sleep on the main highways. Restaurants wouldn't serve us. Teen-age white girls who were serving as car hops would come bouncing out to the car and stop dead when they saw we were Negroes, spin around without a word and walk away.
>
> Some gasoline stations didn't want to sell us gas and oil. Some told us that no rest rooms were available. The looks of anger at the sight of us colored folks sitting in a nice car were frightening to see.
>
> To turn off the main highway and find a place to eat and sleep in a colored neighbourhood meant losing so much time that we finally were driving hundreds of

extra miles each day to get to the next city in which
I was to sing so that we could get a place to eat and
sleep . . . by the time I was supposed to sing I was
almost dizzy.[57]

And because Bessie Smith came from the South and was
killed in Mississippi, the rumours began immediately and
continued for over thirty years. It is not surprising, given
the racism of the segregated South and the drama of Bessie
Smith's own life, that such a story should have survived
many different tellings over all those years. It was initially
sparked off by an article of John Hammond's in *Downbeat*
magazine entitled 'Did Bessie Smith Bleed to Death While
Waiting for Medical Aid?' Here was the terrible sentence
that burned for many years: 'When finally she did arrive
at the hospital she was refused treatment because of her
color and bled to death while waiting for attention.' Once
the article appeared people refused to believe any other
version of events. She *had* died that way. Racism had murdered her. Racism had killed so many black people in the
American South through Jim Crow laws and lynchings;
Bessie Smith was seen as yet one more victim. It is easy to
see why, to imagine that a whites-only hospital might have
been closer by on that road where she had the accident; that
they might have wasted time driving to the Afro-American
Hospital; that the woman travelling in another car which
became involved in the accident might have been treated
more quickly because she was white. The truth is that black

lives in the United States of America at that point in history were not valued, so precious time could easily have been wasted. There's no rush to save a black life. Sidney Bechet said, 'I was told the doctors, they hadn't too much concern for getting to her quick.'[58] People from Mezz Mezzrow to Edward Albee believed the story about her death. Albee was so outraged and moved that he wrote a play about it called *The Death of Bessie Smith*. It was written in 1959 and opened in West Berlin in 1960:

> JACK: Ma'am, I got Bessie Smith out in that car there.
> SECOND NURSE: I don't care who you got out there, nigger. You cool your heels![59]

The image of the racist white nurse is not a joke. It is true. Bessie Smith could have died of racism. The truth about racism has kept the story going. Sadly, for racism to have an impact on the general public it needs to happen to somebody well known enough to matter. There probably were many people who died in road accidents in the South because white hospitals refused to admit them, but not being famous, their names don't stick. Bessie Smith's death became a symbol of racism. It was a warning. Just like her blues were warnings. This could happen to you. The fact that it maybe didn't happen to her is not the point. People believed it had. And in a strange way this is fitting. There was her life, full of fabrications and embellishments and stories galore. And there's her death: more stories.

People tell different stories about Bessie Smith because her life was so dramatic and her death was so tragic. Her blues were sensational. She was the stuff that dreams are made of. She is the real thing. And she is also the unreal thing because her life combines truth and lies so expertly that for years people couldn't tell one from the other, and that is why she remains so fascinating.

Since it was discovered by Chris Albertson, Bessie's first real biographer, that she did not die the victim of white Southern racism, later books on the blues have been keen to point this out. As if the truth mattered. Well, of course it does. But what interests me the most is why it was so important for people to believe for so long that Bessie had died that way. They didn't just want her to be a famous blues singer who died in a car accident, they wanted her to be a martyr. Someone who gave their lifeblood at the scene. She needed to be a proper victim so that she could become a total heroine. Her blues weren't enough. There had to be the onslaught of racism to finish her off. Perhaps people needed to believe Bessie died in this way because it confirmed their own experiences of racism. Perhaps it was a way of telling themselves that what they experienced every day was real as hell. Look, if Bessie Smith, Empress of the Blues, is not admitted to a hospital, then what chance do the rest of us have? They needed somebody big enough to prove that racism was lethal, murderous and totally destructive. It is not surprising therefore that the story continued to circulate for so many years after her death, particularly since the account given by one Dr Smith, who was on the scene a few minutes after the accident, is contradictory. The white woman in the other car was taken away in an ambulance before Bessie Smith, although her injuries were not life-threatening. Coupled with the fact that the doctor didn't drive Bessie Smith to the hospital himself for fear of getting blood in his car, this adds to the terrible picture. Richard Morgan said that he had to walk ten miles to Clarksdale to get an ambulance for Bessie, wasting precious time. It is also difficult to work out why, if the accident occurred at three in the morning, Bessie received no medical aid for over seven hours. Even now, although many books, including the *Blues Who's Who*, state that Bessie's dying at the hands of white racism is untrue, my temptation is to hesitate.

If it is not definitely true that she died as a result of the combined racism of a doctor on the road and doctors at the white hospital in Clarksdale, it is certainly true that nobody bought her a headstone for thirty-three years. *That* is surprising considering the number of affluent stars who knew her. They could tell the stories and write the plays but they did not take the trouble to mark her grave. The stories about Bessie Smith's death had in a sense nothing to do with Bessie Smith; they had everything to do with the white racism of the 1930s. They told a story about Mississippi, not really a story about the Empress although she was the main character in it. This is Mezz Mezzrow's account:

You ever hear what happened to that fine, full-of-
life female woman? You know how she died? . . . one
day in 1937 she was in an automobile crash down
in Mississippi, the Murder State, and her arm was
almost tore out of its socket. They brought her to the
hospital but it seemed like there wasn't any room just
then – the people around there didn't care for the color
of her skin. The car turned around and drove away,
with Bessie's blood dripping on the floor mat. She was
finally admitted to another hospital where the officials
must have been color-blind, but by that time she had
lost so much blood that they couldn't operate on her,
and a little later she died. 'See that lonesome road,
Lawd, it got to end,' she used to sing. That was how
the lonesome road ended up for the greatest folk singer
this country ever heard, with Jim Crow directing the
traffic.[60]

If she didn't die of white racism, what did she die of?
She didn't die of a drugs overdose; she didn't die of liver
failure through alcohol abuse (though she might have, the
amount she put away). She didn't die of a heart attack
while on stage making her comeback, singing a new kind
of blues. Her death was dramatic enough, but maybe too
ordinary. A car accident. She died, not just because she
lost a lot of blood, but because she was in shock. The
shock of having her arm practically severed was what
killed her.

My life was changed by Bessie's blues. My soul *was* converted. Any good art transforms you, makes you ask yourself questions about the world you live in, people, laws, yourself. Any good art can change the way you look at yourself. I will always associate the dawning of my own realisation of being black with the blues, and particularly Bessie's blues. I will always keep the imaginary Bessie that I had from my childhood. I have partly made her up from there on. All our real heroines appear in the strange slow evenings of childhood. With the presumptuousness of a child, I have imagined myself on her journey, travelling with her through the South in that Pullman. Her blues still fill me with a strange comfort, a freedom, a sense of heading out on the road, an admission that I will never really know what road I am on: *You got me going, you got me going, but I don't know where I'm heading for.* There is the wide open road. Sometimes I can't bear to listen to Bessie Smith. Sometimes her voice gives me no escape. Whenever I do listen to her, I am forced to confront myself. She clues me in. The blues know everything. There is nothing in all of life that is not in the blues. The blues know you and they will come and get you in the night. Bessie's blues were like secrets, something special I was being told and would always guard. Blues singers seem to sing out their very heart and soul; they make you listen, pouring your own heart and soul out as you do so. Bessie's blues still fill me with a strange longing. I don't know exactly what for. Blackness? A culture that will wholly embrace me? Belonging? Who knows. But every time I listen to Bessie Smith, I am drawn backwards, downwards into myself. Every time I listen, I remember something, myself as a young girl, somebody who has disappointed me, some betrayal. The blues don't allow you to forget anything. Every cheating man is remembered, every dirty no-gooder, every unmarked grave. And the amazing thing about the blues is that they tell you not once, twice, but repeatedly the same truth over and over. The blues are not frightened of repetition. In fact repetition is the secret of the blues, the key to their long-lasting success. What goes round comes round. The blues are circular, which is why people will keep on listening to them, round and round. Bessie Smith will alternate through time, being very popular at one moment and not so at another, depending on circumstance and fashion, but she will never die out. A true voice is immortal. In the words of Paul Oliver: 'Bessie Smith was destined to be the greatest Negro recording artist of her day and one of the most outstanding figures in the whole history of American music.'[61]

Bessie Smith's unique voice will continue to haunt us for the next millennium. Her voice sums up the twentieth century. Patrick O'Connor, while he was editor of *Opera News*, said he believed Smith was, 'in fact, the most important musical voice of the twentieth century'.[62] Alberta Hunter wrote:

But Bessie Smith was the greatest of them all. There never was one like her and there will never be one like her again. Even though she was raucous and loud, she had a sort of a tear – no, not a tear, but there was a misery in what she did. It was as though there was something she had to get out, something she just had to bring to the fore. Nobody, least of all today, could ever match Bessie Smith.[63]

Here is a woman, born poor in Chattanooga, Tennessee, started singing on street corners at the age of nine, joined the Rabbit Foot Minstrels at the age of nineteen, and by the time she was twenty-nine was selling 780,000 copies of 'Downhearted Blues' within six months. Here is a woman who took the record company Columbia by storm, making over 160 recordings and singing with the best musicians of her day – Louis Armstrong, Don Redman, Fred Longshaw, Fletcher Henderson, Jack Teagarden, Benny Goodman.

As it says on the headstone, which was a long time coming:

## THE GREATEST BLUES SINGER IN THE WORLD WILL NEVER STOP SINGING

I force myself to imagine her real death. The one she had. The accident itself. What might have been going through her head. It is a peculiar way of getting even closer to her. It is a strange thing to do. Somehow the death of the famous activates the popular imagination. The deaths of Martin Luther King, Malcolm X, Billie Holiday, Bob Marley are all epic, grand-scale deaths. Perhaps somebody is not truly famous unless their death is also extraordinary, unusual, horrific in small and large details, gruesome and terrifying to the core of the human heart. The life of every true hero is bent on ending in tragedy. Heroes can't help themselves. *Show me a hero and I'll show you a tragedy.*

*The car accident happened in slow motion. Her death was in slow motion. So slow her life is going before her, just like she heard them say it did. She is herself, on roller skates, the pair she thinks she bought herself when her mother was still alive with her first wages from the Ivory Theatre, Chattanooga, back in those days with Ma Rainey and Fat Chappelle's Rabbit Foot Minstrels. But she suddenly remembers, as the car slowly, slowly hits that truck, that her mother herself was dead before she ever sang on stage and that all her life she's made her mother up in places where she didn't really exist. Her mother has come with her all along, in and out of all those tents, in and out of all those studios. She goes to try and take her hand. She is terrified of dying. She thinks to herself, don't let anyone tell you this is easy, then she realises she won't be around to tell anyone it wasn't. That's why no one really knows except the ghosts who don't talk the same language anyway. That's it in a crunch, the point of her whole life, the meaning of her whole life is this death. It's like she was coming towards it forever, this particular death. Not a heart attack on the stage of Beale Street Palace or Liberty Theatre or Lincoln Theatre or any of those others. Not slowly disintegrating with some wasting-away disease. Not asleep in bed. Not giving birth to a baby. She was never going to lie down and die peacefully; she was going to be destroyed. Her death was always going to be dangerous. She knew that. She knew that all along. She's waiting for somebody in that truck to fire a shotgun. Or for a man to appear and stab her with a knife. She's been stabbed before. She could have died that time. No, it always was going to be on the road, in a car accident. On the road going to a theatre. Driving on the road. Her whole life has been on the road or on the rails. Up and down and across this whole fucking country. Ain't a town she can't put her finger on. A list of every theatre she has ever performed in flashes up on the windscreen of the automobile as it slowly, slowly approaches that parked truck. Beale Street Palace, Memphis. Koppin Theatre, Detroit. Globe Theatre, Cleveland. Orpheum Theatre, Nashville. Franklin Theatre, Birmingham. Roosevelt Theatre, Cincinnati. Standard Theatre, Philadelphia. The Nest Club, NYC. Lafayette Theatre, NYC. Grand Theatre, Chicago. Howard Theatre, Washington, DC. Liberty Theatre, Chattanooga. Ivory Theatre, Chattanooga. Chattanooga, Chattanooga.*

*Chattanooga. That's where she's heading for. She can see herself on the corner of Ninth Street. She can see herself walking down Charles Street. That was some one-room ramshackle cabin. That cabin seemed smaller than this car that is heading for that truck. There is no escape. She is terrified. She knows what's happening. Her*

*arm is hanging out of the car and she can't get it back in.*
*Richard's hands are slow and thick on the wheel. She can*
*see he can't do nothing. He's trying to turn the wheel fast*
*to the right. She sees two tiny beads of sweat appear on his*
*knuckles. He's shouting and she thinks she is shouting too.*
*Her voice is loud as a horn outside of herself.*

*You don't accept it. You don't accept that it is yourself*
*dying at first. You think he's got the wrong woman. He's*
*picked the wrong number, that dirty no-gooder up in that*
*fucking sky. What've you done? Why didn't he get Jack*
*Gee first? Why not Clarence Williams? You been reckless*
*and you wasted your life; you beat up some people who had*
*it coming. And you didn't try and get your boy back. You*
*didn't go hunting for him. Why didn't you go hunting for*
*him? Why didn't you try and get Jack back? Now you see*
*him and he's five and it's the first time you met him and*
*you made up your mind then, you was going to adopt that*
*boy, Snooks, going to be yours. There he was in Macon,*
*Georgia, looking at you like he loved you. Did he? Did*
*anyone love you? Did Tinnie, Viola, Laura, Clarence,*
*Andrew, Lulu? Did Earl Love, Jack Gee, Ruby Walker,*
*Lillian what's her name, did any of them love you? It*
*doesn't matter now. It doesn't matter at all. When you*
*are heading for death, these things fall off you like layers*
*of skin. You are like a snake in the end, shedding those*
*memories faster than skindust. It's all falling off. The blues*
*are falling off the truck. The blues you sang seemed to*
*order your whole life for you. In the House Blues, Sweet*

*Potato Blues, Safety Mama; Backwater Blues, Lonesome Desert Blues, Young Woman's Blues, Downhearted Blues, It Makes My Love Come Down, Spider Man Blues, My Man Blues, Foolish Man Blues, Dirty No-Gooder Blues, Please Help Me Get Him Off My Mind, Jail House Blues, Reckless Blues, Wasted Life Blues, Rocking Chair Blues. These are the ones you wrote yourself. You remember them better; the words fall individually now from the front of the truck onto the front of your car: That man put somethin' on me; oh, take it off me please. The avaricious face of Jack Gee bent over a pile of your money, counting, counting, twists itself towards you as the car upturns. You don't forgive people as you are dying. Don't let anybody say you do. You just wipe them out, one by one, like you had one big duster in your hand. The faces left at the end, those are the faces that matter. You can't get that bastard Jack Gee wiped out completely. You can still see the top of his square head and those eyes of his. Ruby is just behind him. There's even more of her left. She's got her whole face and the top of her shoulders. Just behind Ruby in the distance are Ma and Pa standing in the rain. One last look at Ma's gold teeth. As if you needed to!*

*But the strange thing is a whole gang of people you haven't seen for years gathers round you when your arm practically comes off. The last thing you see are those faces from Chattanooga way back when you were a girl. Your mother is still young. And you are her angel child. She has got your arm and she is keeping it. She could stitch that arm back on herself if she was really alive you think. And that is nearly your last thought. Then you think hell, I ain't never thought death would be like this. You ain't never thought death would get you to thinking about all of this stuff. When you are dying you think fast on your back and you can get in more thoughts in those dying minutes than you've thought your whole life and you suddenly get a chance to see yourself different. Shit, you even get a chance to see yourself dying. Not just see yourself dying, 'cause that isn't important any more. Visual things aren't important when the crunch comes. You feel yourself going down, like you going down underneath the world, swirling, doing the Black Bottom, all the way down. Your feet don't stop moving. You start to stomp. You lying there on the road covered in your own blood and at the same time you are dancing down to death. And then everything goes dark but the noise continues. You don't see your own death coming; you hear it. It is not just one loud noise; it's a whole gang of noise, shouting, barrelhousing, cussing, crashing, cutting piano, stomping, snare-drumming, car-screeching, glass-shattering, tyres-screaming, car-weeping noise. Death is loud. Don't let anybody tell you different. You ain't never heard such shit.*

*That's the way it is. It is rough and dark. Don't let anybody tell you any different. And where does that lonesome road take you? It takes you all the way down to hell. You knew you was never going no place else.*

Feeling tomorrow like I feel today,
Feeling tomorrow like I feel today,
I pack my grip and make my getaway . . .

'St Louis Blues'

*The great thing about hell is the parties. Hell's parties*
*are rough and dark, way, way better than Harlem's.*
*They've got pigs' feet here you ain't seen in your wildest*
*dreams and beer to wash them down with that you ain't*
*tasted in your sweet life, dancing so fast you can't see your*
*feet touch the rims of hell. They still do the camel, the*
*shimmy, the bo hog, the skate and the buzzard here, only*
*they don't call them that. They don't have any language in*
*hell. No fucking words at all. It's all sensations. They feed*
*you well and they dance you well and when you get to sing*
*you raise hell. A lot of the old blues people are whooping it*
*up. Well, well beyond the break of day.*

# THUMBNAIL SKETCH

1894 Born 15 April, Chattanooga, Hamilton County, Tennessee. Father: William Smith, a Baptist minister. Mother: Laura Smith. Born into poverty, one of eight children. Both parents died before she was nine.

1903 Sang on the corner of Ninth Street for pennies.

1912 Joined the Moses Stokes Travelling Show as a dancer. Ma Rainey and Pa Rainey were part of the troupe.

1912–21 Toured the South gathering a huge live audience. Worked with the Rabbit Foot Minstrels, the Florida Cotton Blossoms, Silas Green's Minstrel Show.

1918 Appeared in her own show, *Liberty Belles Revue*, at 91 Theatre, Atlanta as singer, dancer, male impersonator.

1920 Married her first husband, Earl Love, who died a year later.

1923 Appeared with Sidney Bechet in musical comedy *How Come* at Dunbar Theatre, Philadelphia. Turned down by Okeh Records for being 'too rough'. Made her first record, 'Downhearted Blues', with Columbia Records. It sold a record-breaking 780,000 copies in six months. Married Jack Gee, her second husband. Met Ruby Walker.

1923–31 Recorded extensively with Columbia Records on an exclusive contract, 160 songs in all. At her peak, in 1925, Columbia paid her $200 per usable side.

1925 Bought her own Pullman railroad car.
– 14 January: recorded 'St Louis Blues' with Louis Armstrong.

1926 Legally adopted Snooks, renaming him Jack Gee Junior.

1929 Separated from Jack Gee.
– 15 May: recorded 'Nobody Knows You When You're Down and Out'.
– June: appeared in film *St Louis Blues*.

1931 Dropped by Columbia. Started relationship with Chicago bootlegger Richard Morgan.

1933 Recorded 'Gimme a Pigfoot', 'Do Your Duty', 'Take Me for a Buggy Ride' and her swansong, 'Down in the Dumps', with Okeh Records, receiving just $37 per usable side.

1930–37 Earned a living touring the South again with her own show, *Bessie Smith Revue*.

1937 26 September: Bessie Smith died in a car crash on Route 61, Clarksdale, Mississippi.

# NOTES

1 Chris Albertson, *Bessie*, Stein & Day, New York, 1971
2 Donald Clarke, *Wishing on the Moon: The Life and Times of Billie Holiday*, Viking, London, 1974
3 Will Friedwald, *Jazz Singing*, Da Capo, New York, 1996
4 W. C. Handy, *Father of the Blues: An Autobiography*, Macmillan, New York, 1941; Da Capo, New York, 1985
5 Richard Newman, *Everybody Say Freedom: Everything You Need to Know About African-American History*, Plume, New York, 1996
6 Albertson, *Bessie*
7 Paul Oliver, *Songsters and Saints: Vocal Traditions on Race Records*, Cambridge University Press, Cambridge, 1984
8 Sally Placksin, *Jazzwomen: 1900 to the Present*, Pluto Press, London, 1985
9 ibid.
10 ibid.
11 Albertson, *Bessie*
12 Sidney Bechet, *Treat It Gentle*, Hill and Wang, New York, 1960; Da Capo, New York, 2002
13 Nat Shapiro and Nat Hentoff, *Hear Me Talkin' to Ya: The Story of Jazz as Told by the Men Who Made It*, Dover, New York, 1966
14 ibid.
15 Albertson, *Bessie*
16 ibid.
17 ibid.
18 ibid.

19  ibid.

20  ibid.

21  Humphrey Lyttelton, *The Best of Jazz*, Robson Books, London, 1978

22  Albertson, *Bessie*

23  Placksin, *Jazzwomen*

24  Chris Albertson, Notes to *Bessie Smith: The Complete Recordings*, Columbia, 1991

25  Alan Lomax, *The Land Where the Blues Began*, Methuen, London, 1993

26  Michele Wallace, *Invisibility Blues*, Verso, New York, 1990

27  Oliver, *Songsters and Saints*

28  Shapiro and Hentoff, *Hear Me Talkin' to Ya*

29  ibid.

30  Hettie Jones, *Big Star Fallin' Mama*, Viking, New York, 1974

31  Lyttelton, *The Best of Jazz*

32  Geneviève Fabre and Robert O'Meally (eds), *History and Memory in African-American Culture*, Oxford University Press, New York, 1995

33  Shapiro and Hentoff, *Hear Me Talkin' to Ya*

34  Lyttelton, *The Best of Jazz*

35  Oliver, *Songsters and Saints*

36  Albertson, *Bessie*

37  ibid.

38  ibid.

39  ibid.

40  ibid.

41  Shapiro and Hentoff, *Hear Me Talkin' to Ya*

42  ibid.

43  Jervis Anderson, *Harlem: The Great Black Way*, Orbis Publishing, London, 1972

44  Albertson, *Bessie*

45  Philip Furia, *Poets of Tin Pan Alley: A History of America's Great Lyricists*, Oxford University Press, New York, 1990

46  Handy, *Father of the Blues*

47  Albert Murray, *Stomping the Blues*, Da Capo, New York, 1989

48  Friedwald, *Jazz Singing*

49  Clarke, *Wishing on the Moon*

50  Albertson, *Bessie*

51  ibid.

52  ibid.

53  Newman, *Everybody Say Freedom*

54  Albertson, *Bessie*

55  *Cashbox* Magazine, 1966

56  Lomax, *The Land Where the Blues Began*

57  Mahalia Jackson, *Movin' On Up*, Hawthorn Books, 1966

58  Bechet, *Treat It Gentle*

59  Edward Albee, *The Death of Bessie Smith*, First Plume, New York, 1988

60  Mezz Mezzrow in Shapiro and Hentoff, *Hear Me Talkin' to Ya*

61  Oliver, *Songsters and Saints*

62  Newman, *Everybody Say Freedom*

63  Shapiro and Hentoff, *Hear Me Talkin' to Ya*

# SELECTED READING

Albee, Edward, *The Death of Bessie Smith*, First Plume, New York, 1988

Albertson, Chris, *Bessie*, Stein & Day, New York, 1971

Anderson, Jervis, *Harlem: The Great Black Way*, Orbis Publishing, London, 1972

Armstrong, Louis, *Satchmo: My Life in New Orleans*, Da Capo, New York, 1986

Bechet, Sidney, *Treat It Gentle*, Hill and Wang, New York, 1960

Clarke, Donald, *Wishing on the Moon: The Life and Times of Billie Holiday*, Viking, London, 1974

Dahl, Linda, *Stormy Weather: The Music and Lives of a Century of Jazzwomen*, Quartet, London, 1984

Fabre, Geneviève, and O'Meally, Robert (eds), *History and Memory in African-American Culture*, Oxford University Press, New York, 1995

Friedwald, Will, *Jazz Singing*, Da Capo, New York, 1996

Furia, Philip, *Poets of Tin Pan Alley: A History of America's Great Lyricists*, Oxford University Press, New York, 1990

Garon, Paul, *Blues and the Poetic Spirit*, City Lights, San Francisco, 1975

Garon, Paul, and Garon, Beth, *Woman with Guitar: Memphis Minnie's Blues*, Da Capo, New York, 1992

Handy, W. C., *Father of the Blues: An Autobiography*, Macmillan, New York, 1941; Da Capo, New York, 1985

Harris, Sheldon, *Blues Who's Who*, Da Capo, New York, 1991

Lomax, Alan, *The Land Where the Blues Began*, Methuen, London, 1993

# SELECTED READING

Lyttelton, Humphrey, *The Best of Jazz*, Robson Books, London, 1978

Murray, Albert, *Stomping the Blues*, Da Capo, New York, 1976

Newman, Richard, *Everybody Say Freedom: Everything You Need to Know About African-American History*, Plume, New York, 1996

Oliver, Paul, *Songsters and Saints: Vocal Traditions on Race Records*, Cambridge University Press, Cambridge, 1984

Placksin, Sally, *Jazzwomen: 1900 to the Present*, Pluto Press, London, 1985

Shapiro, Nat, and Hentoff, Nat, *Hear Me Talkin' to Ya: The Story of Jazz as Told by the Men Who Made It*, Dover, New York, 1966

White, Newman, *American Negro Folk Songs*, Folklore, Pennsylvania, 1965

# CREDITS

## LYRICS

Bourne Music Ltd.: 'Mistreatin' Daddy' by Porter Grainger and Bob Ricketts, copyright © Bourne Music Ltd. (renewed). International copyright secured. All rights reserved. Reprinted by permission of Bourne Music Ltd.

Hal Leonard Europe Limited: Excerpt from 'Florida Bound', words and music by Clarence Williams. Copyright © 1925 by Universal Music Corp. (renewed). All rights reserved. Excerpt from 'Wild Women Don't Get the Blues', words and music by Ida Cox. Copyright © 1924 by Universal Music Corp. (renewed). All rights reserved. Excerpt from 'T'aint Nobody's Bizness', words and music by Porter Grainger and Everett Robbins. All rights for World excluding United States and Canada: Copyright © 1922 by Universal Music Corp., copyright renewed. All rights reserved. Reprinted by permission of Hal Leonard Europe Limited.

Hal Leonard Europe Limited and Round Hill Carlin (London): Excerpt from 'Strange Fruit', words and music by Lewis Allan. Copyright © 1939 by Edward B. Marks Music Company, copyright renewed 1995 by Music Sales Corporation. All rights for World excluding United States are controlled by Edward B. Marks Music Company. For the United States: Copyright © 1939 by Music Sales Corporation (renewed). International copyright secured. All rights reserved. Reprinted by permission of Hal Leonard Europe Limited and Round Hill Carlin (London).